PRIMER contents

growing
gospel-driven
churches

 **fiec** ◆ the **FELLOWSHIP** of **INDEPENDENT EVANGELICAL CHURCHES**

Primer is produced by the Fellowship of Independent Evangelical Churches (FIEC); a family of churches in Britain, working together to go and make disciples of Jesus Christ in every community. Find out more at *fiec.org.uk*

1

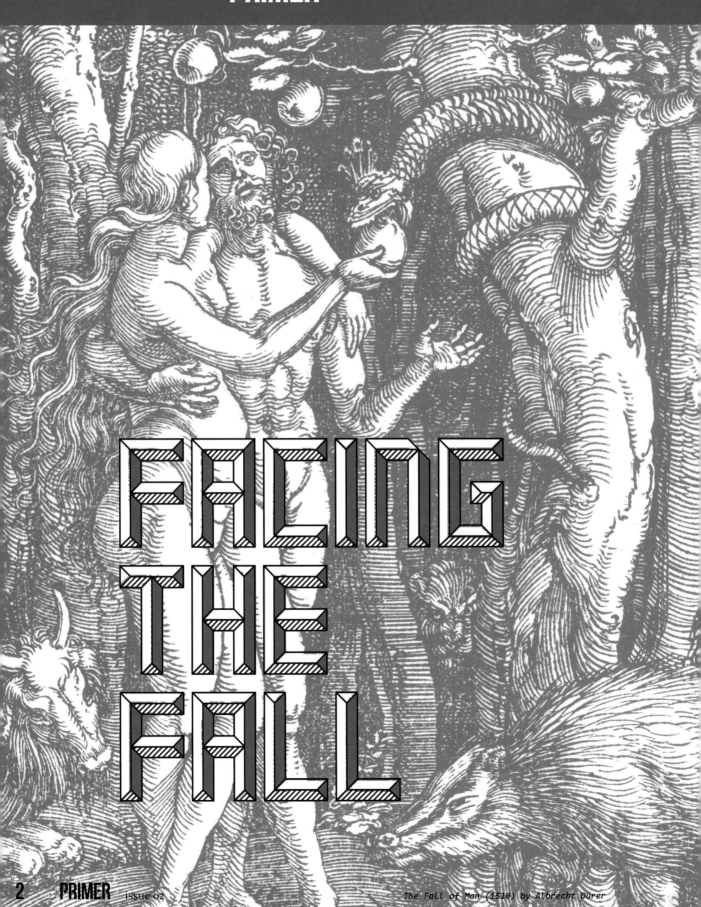

FACING THE FALL

The Fall of Man (1510) by Albrecht Dürer

As one of the articles in this issue of *Primer* says, *"Pastoral ministry brings you face to face with sin."* We face the fall every day. And yet it is often so hard to help people (us included) to really grasp the reality and gravity of sin. That's true for lots of reasons.

In our evangelism, we come up against a society largely in denial about sin. To take just one example, last year *The Guardian* ran an article by George Monbiot called *'We're Not as Selfish as We Think We Are. Here's the Proof.'* And here's the "proof":

> *A large majority of the 1,000 people they surveyed – 74% – identifies more strongly with unselfish values than with selfish values. This means that they are more interested in helpfulness, honesty, forgiveness and justice than in money, fame, status and power. The second is that a similar majority – 78% – believes others to be more selfish than they really are. In other words, we have made a terrible mistake about other people's minds.*

George Monbiot, 'We're Not as Selfish as We Think We Are. Here's the Proof,' *The Guardian*, October 14, 2015, sec. Opinion, www.theguardian.com/ commentisfree/2015/oct/14/ selfish-proof-ego-humans- inherently-good

Put simply, I'm not as bad as you might think (you can take my word for that), and you're not as bad as I think you are. We make mistakes. We have lapses, errors of judgment. But we aren't fallen, at worst we stumble.

So there is denial about our own sin, but then we are often very quick to see sin in others and to blame others for all sorts of things: *they* are the reason we're in this mess, *they* are out to get us. By way of illustration, there was a fascinating moment on an episode of the BBC's *Newsnight* after the 2008 banking crisis. The villains of that moment of course were the bankers, but the former Archbishop of Canterbury Rowan Williams suggested we needed "corporate self-examination" to explain why we were seduced by a consumerist mindset. When he suggested the answer had something to do with original sin the host Jeremy Paxman spluttered controllably. "You don't really believe that do you?!" The former Archbishop persevered, but in that wider discussion he was a lone voice crying in the wilderness. The general consensus was that either a group ('fat cat city bankers') or an abstraction ('capitalism'/'deregularization') was to blame. Someone or something was to blame, but it certainly wasn't us.

news.bbc.co.uk/1/hi/programmes/ newsnight/8259172.stm

And what about sin as a theme in our ministry? How much do we face up to the fall? Well, many readers of *Primer* will be used to speaking about sin regularly, even emphasising it. But there is a danger that we become a bit one dimensional – defaulting to one way of explaining sin, one go-to framework or illustration. Other times we can be aware that our Protestant heritage comes with terms like 'total depravity' which are often misunderstood and easily left to one side. Or then there are pastoral situations where it can be so hard to disentangle a person's responsibility for their own sin from a matrix of addiction, compulsive behaviour, and the grip of their upbringing.

For those reasons *Primer* issue 02 takes sin as its theme. In different ways the first three articles help us to wrestle with the depth and breadth of how the Bible describes sin. First, Graham Beynon reflects on the ways in which several recent books distil the essence of sin and draws out some helpful ministry implications for us.

Next, Tim Ward turns a spotlight on the ways in which we characteristically preach about sin to unbelievers and believers. It's the article equivalent of a rigorous back massage: you'll feel like you've been prodded in a few uncomfortable ways, but you'll get up off the table feeling in much better shape.

Third, we have reprinted a section from the *Institutes* by John ('total depravity') Calvin. The reason for choosing this passage for our historical text segment is that we find Calvin at his best here. He offers a powerful account of sin's utter grip on human beings, and yet he does so in a nuanced way that can account for goodness in the world and in a pastoral way which leads to a deeper sense of wonder, for salvation is necessarily God's gift to us. To help us through that, Mark Troughton is our guide, introducing and annotating the text.

The final three articles have a more practical focus. Kirsten Birkett tackles the subject of addiction, bringing together medical and theological perspectives in a rare but crucial combination. Next we have a Q&A with theologian John Frame. You may know him as the author of very big books, but here he gives short and clear answers to a number of questions about sin submitted by followers of *@PrimerHQ* on Twitter. Lastly, I'll share some thoughts on the ways in which our society functions as a *victim* culture; shifting blame onto others and protesting our innocence. We'll reflect on what this victim culture reveals about sin, and how we can respond in our church life and evangelism.

DAVID SHAW is the Editor of *Primer*. He is part-time Theological Adviser for FIEC and part-time lecturer in New Testament and Greek at Oak Hill Theological College, London. He's married to Jo and they have four children.

 @_david_shaw

GRAHAM BEYNON is pastor of Grace Church, Cambridge, and also Director of Independent Ministry Training at Oak Hill College. His PhD was from St Andrews University examining the theology of Isaac Watts and he is also the author of a number of books.

KIRSTEN BIRKETT teaches ethics and philosophy at Oak Hill College, and is a Latimer Research Fellow. She has written several books on the relationship between Christianity and science as well as psychology, feminism and church history.

JOHN CALVIN trained as a lawyer before becoming a leading theologian and pastor of the Reformation. He was married to Idelette and was the author of many commentaries, sermons, and, most famously, the *Institutes of the Christian Religion*.

JOHN FRAME is J. D. Trimble Prof. of Systematic Theology and Philosophy at Reformed Theological Seminary, Orlando, FL. He has authored many books, including *Systematic Theology* and *A History of Western Philosophy and Theology*.

 @DrJohnFrame

MARK TROUGHTON taught French, Italian and English for 10 years before retraining for church ministry. He went to Switzerland in 1994, where he worked as a pastor, trainer, Bible teacher and church planter. Mark has been pastor of York Evangelical Church since February 2004.

 @TroughtoMark

TIM WARD has served as Associate Director of The Proclamation Trust Cornhill Training Course since 2013. Before that he was in pastoral ministry for 14 years as an ordained Anglican.

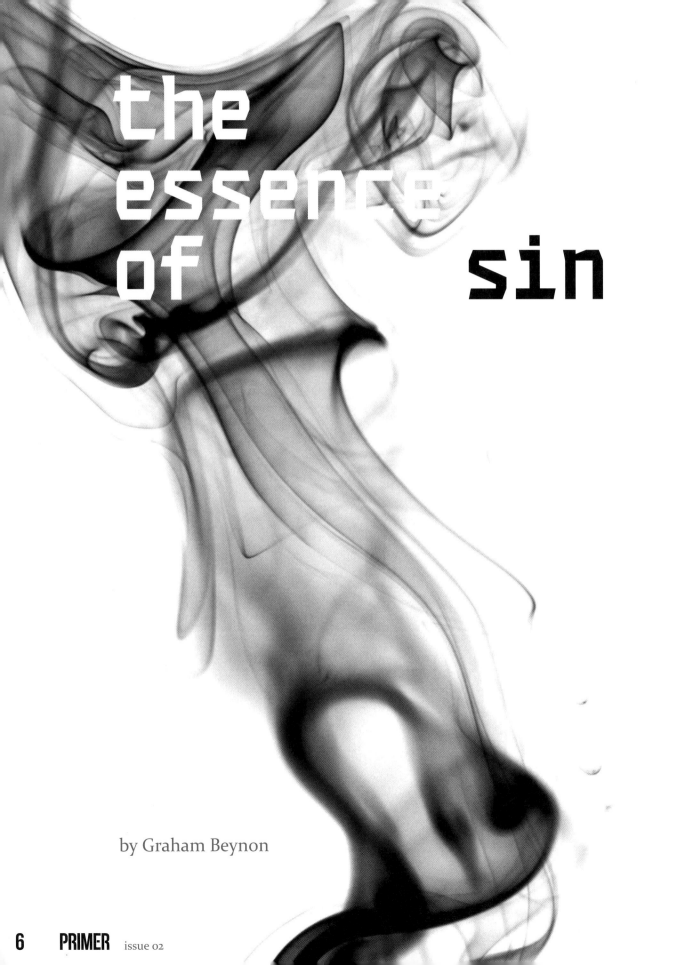

the essence of sin

sin

by Graham Beynon

Pastoral ministry brings you face to face with sin.

You see its presence, its pervasiveness, and the destruction it wreaks in people's lives.

You see the many varieties of sin: sin in attitudes and actions, silent sins in people's hearts and verbal sins from their mouths, sins of religious subtlety and sins of overt ungodliness.

You see the effects of sin in the corrosion of trust, distortions of relationships, and poisoning of all that is good and right.

You see these things in the lives you minister to, and of course you see the same things within yourself.

We can add that for those of us in church leadership, many ministerial sins will also be stirred up within us: pride, self-pity, cowardice, and more. Time in pastoral ministry is time looking at the multi-coloured horror of sin.

But if you were to put every sin in a pot and boil them all down, would there be one clear ingredient left at the end?

Is there an *essence* of sin?

This article will review and discuss a number of recent books on the topic of sin. What is being attempted are not full book 'reviews' – there are many aspects of these books that will not be mentioned. Rather it's a discussion of this key topic which features in each of them in different ways: what is the essence of sin?

That's a question worth for asking for several reasons. First, it will help us see a *unity* in Scripture. We must never make the multi-coloured picture of sin in Scripture monochrome. But if there is an essence behind the various pictures given, then we will see them and teach them as a unity, rather than as a pick-and-mix variety.

Secondly, we will be able to *apply* the doctrine of sin more readily to a variety of people. When we read that people are 'filled with every kind of wickedness, evil, greed and depravity' (Rom 1:29), not everyone will immediately think it describes them. Some people are genuinely quite pleasant. But they are still sinners, and seeing the essence of sin will help us show them how that is so.

Thirdly, we will be able to *help* people in sanctification with greater clarity. Understanding the essence of sin, its internal dynamics, will guide us in how to fight it; and to do so at a fundamental rather than a superficial level.

So what is the essence to sin?

To start with here is a brief introduction to each book:

Missing the Mark: Sin and Its Consequences in Biblical Theology
Mark E. Biddle (Abingdon Press, 2005)

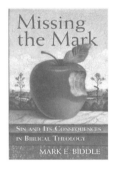

Biddle is concerned that the traditional conception of sin as rebellion doesn't appreciate its complexity. So along with sin as wilful rebellion he also argues for sin as a failure to embrace authentic humanity (explained more below). Behind both these manifestations of sin is a more fundamental mistrust of God. Along with this Biddle examines the consequences of sin in Scripture: he sees it has having significant organic 'after effects' and contributing to systems of sin in society, much of which he believes the Church has failed to recognise. All of this is seen as important in pastoral ministry today. Biddle works off multiple biblical texts often tracing a theme helpfully through Scripture. He also draws on insights from psychology and sociology.

Fallen: A Theology of Sin
Edited by Christopher W. Morgan and Robert A. Peterson (Crossway, 2013)

This is a multiple author book covering biblical, systematic and pastoral issues. As usual with such books it does not have a single thesis and so is difficult to summarise. Biblical chapters examine the understanding of sin in sections of Scripture (Law, Prophets, Paul, etc.) Some of these are slightly idiosyncratic in approach but still helpful; Doug Moo on sin in Paul is excellent. The systematic and pastoral chapters are good overviews with many helpful insights. On the downside there can be a feeling of repetitiveness between them as the same introductory ground is often covered.

Not the Way It's Supposed to Be: A Breviary of Sin

Cornelius Plantinga, Jr (Eerdmans, 1995)

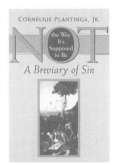

This is a very thoughtful and stimulating book giving a contemporary account of sin. Plantinga tends to work off metaphors (e.g. 'pollution') and to tell stories, rather than expound the biblical text. But that is only to comment on his approach rather than to suggest the content is unbiblical. The greatest strength of the book is the vivid portrayal of the working of sin, its subtleties, ironies, and devastating outcomes.

The Doctrine of Sin: In Reformed and Neo-Orthodox Thought

Iain D. Campbell (Christian Focus, 1999)

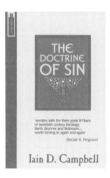

This is an examination of neo-orthodox thought (Barth, Bultmann and Brunner) in the light of biblical and Reformed teaching. Campbell gives a condensed biblical account of sin and then an overview of the hamartiology of the Reformers and later theologians in the Reformed tradition. This fills approximately the first half of the book which then functions as a basis for the examination of neo-orthodox thought that follows. Barth, Bultmann and Brunner in turn are shown to fall short of the Reformed position. It is very informative but probably tries to cover too much ground.

Campbell summarises neo-orthodoxy as an attempt to return to something more objective than culture or personal experience; to emphasise the objectivity of divine revelation' (p13). It was a reaction to 19th century liberalism and in some ways a recovery of Reformed emphases on God, Scripture and human sin. The major figures in the movement, however, are by no means uniform in their views, and none of them slot very easily into the Reformed tradition.

'The theology of sin,' from the Greek word *hamartia* (sin).

The Gravity of Sin

Matt Jenson (T & T Clark, 2006)

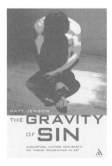

This is an exploration of Luther's conception of sin as humanity 'curved in on itself'. It begins with Augustine's view of sin as misdirected love which Jenson sees as a precursor to Luther's thought. It then examines Luther himself, considers a feminist critique of Luther, and finally explores Barth's expansion of this concept of sin. It argues that this is a helpful umbrella metaphor for sin for today. Examination of each author's thought is detailed and, although well written, does not make for easy reading (it was originally a PhD thesis).

All of the authors are clear on the importance of the topic of sin. It is what has gone wrong with the world; it is the problem to which Christ is the solution. As such it is central to the story of the Bible and deserves close inspection. The authors are probably also agreed on what a difficult topic sin is to pin down. The biblical picture has both great richness and variety, and, in some areas, lack of explanation. Despite this each in their own way give their 'take' on sin. While it is not always central to the argument of the book there is discussion of the essence of sin.

For example the *Westminster Shorter Catechism*:

Q 14: What is sin?
A: Sin is any want of conformity unto, or transgression of, the law of God.

Campbell is clear that within the Reformed tradition sin is seen as lawbreaking and that this is central in the biblical picture. This is one of many areas for which he castigates neo-orthodoxy. One of Campbell's main concerns is the neo-orthodox tendency to minimise sin and reduce it to a form of existential malfunctioning. That is to say he believes the focus moves to the horizontal aspects of sin, (how I relate to others), and to the internal aspects of sin (how I relate to myself). Campbell sees these moves as resulting in a subjective rather than objective understanding of sin. The law in his mind is the biblical bulwark which prevents such a move. So he says that the law under the old covenant gave a measure and standard to judge sin. As a result the law 'externalised sin, as a reminder to the covenant community that sin meant more than a subjective disintegration. It issues in a particular relationship and standing before God.' (p67).

In discussing Reformed theologians' views of sin Campbell shows that lawbreaking is a key element in their thought – along with other emphases such as Adamic headship, the slavery of sin, and total corruption. For example Charles Hodge defines sin in terms of behaviour 'lacking the conformity to the law of God which the Bible demands' (p121). In discussing John Murray's thought Campbell says that 'the pervasiveness of God's law means that supreme standard by which sin is to be judged is the giving of a command on the part of God' (p129). There are similar comments for other theologians.

On the way through his survey Campbell touches on other definitions of sin that have been given. For example Calvin said sin was motivated by pride but more specifically that Eve was led away by unbelief. Luther was similar: he identified the 'root and source of all sin', as 'unbelief in the inmost heart' (p91). Campbell quotes these ideas but does not pursue them or relate them to lawbreaking. To be fair to Campbell he is giving a condensed account of theologians, and he isn't focussing on the essence of sin as his key topic. My point is only that the emphasis on lawbreaking doesn't reflect all that might be said in this overview.

Of course in focussing on lawbreaking Campbell is on safe ground with verses such as 1 John 3:4: 'Everyone who sins breaks the law; in fact, sin is lawlessness.' Similarly, Paul refers to Adam's act of sin which broke a command (Rom 5:14). Questions arise, however: in 1 John 'lawlessness' seems to refer to, or at least reflect, an attitude to the law such as rebellion, and so might not that attitude be more fundamental? In Paul there is discussion of those who sin in a different way to Adam suggesting there's more than one type of sin or, at least, that the law brings an additional element to sin rather than defining it completely (see Rom 5:13-14). In his critique of neo-orthodox theologians Campbell is almost certainly right that they end up minimising sin but I'm not convinced an emphasis on law is the only, or even the main, response.

It is worth noting that Campbell also critiques Tim Keller for his 'rebranding' of sin. Keller uses terminology that he feels resonates more immediately with today's culture such as idolatry, lostness, and self-centredness. Campbell's key concern is again the lack of emphasis on sin as lawbreaking resulting in what he regards as an overly subjective view of sin. There are two questions here: first, What is sin? Second, What is the best way to teach sin in today's culture? These are related but distinct questions. Campbell would presumably answer both of them with 'lawbreaking'. As we will see in a moment I think there is more that can be said.

See his chapter in *Engaging with Keller* (Darlington: Evangelical Press, 2013).

What is helpful about Campbell's highlighting of the law is that it gives a concreteness to sin. Lines are crossed. Laws are broken. Such acts of disobedience to what God has commanded must never be excluded from our understanding of sin. In our culture reference to 'lawbreaking' may sound stark and old fashioned and as a result it is easily played down. You'll have to decide if that means we should deliberately play it up as a counter balance, or if there are better ways to discuss sin today. But while it might not be the picture of sin we begin with, it certainly must not be lost. There is truth to the idea of sin as subjective disintegration, but there is also an objective component to sin which the law pinpoints.

That said, the Scriptures give us ample reason to add to this picture. Why do we transgress the law? What lies behind our acts of lawbreaking? We should note here that the original or first sin in the Bible comes in the form of a narrative which clearly involves the breaking of a command but it also includes details of motive. 'The woman saw that the fruit of the tree was good for food and pleasing to the eye, and also desirable for gaining wisdom...' (Gen 3:6). In that statement and the preceding conversation with the serpent is a wealth of material on the dynamics of sin.

This is where **Jenson** goes in a very different direction to Campbell – not least in how he ends up understanding Barth. Jenson's book focuses on Luther's understanding of sin as *homo incurvatus in se* – that is humanity curved in on itself. This is described as having a 'gravitational' effect where we attempt to draw others into our orbit. Jenson's argument is that: 'the image of being "curved in on oneself" is the best paradigm for understanding sin relationally, that it has sufficient explanatory breadth and depth to be of service to contemporary Christian theology.' (p4).

Augustine is seen to have prepared the way for this understanding with his view of love redirected from God to ourselves. This defines sin relationally rather than substantially: evil is not a thing but the way a will is directed and ordered. Luther develops this idea seeing sin as the focus on self, for self. This means we can even be religious for sinful reasons where we pursue God but for our own ends. Hence sin is far more than lawbreaking – indeed on this understanding we can obey the law sinfully. Within Luther this incurvature is linked to pride.

Jenson then uses Barth to expand on this idea and show how the 'inward turn' can account for a variety of manifestations of sin. Barth spoke of sin having 'different dimensions and aspects', but that it is 'single entity'. Barth sees two key dimensions of sin as pride and sloth, the latter being the self-protective withdrawal into self, a form of culpable negligence.

Jenson also interacts with feminist thinkers who have said that sin as prideful self-focus is true of men but not of women. Women, they argue, are more self-hating than self-exalting; their problem is a failure of self-actualisation (an interesting argument given Eve's lead role in Gen 3). Jenson is (rightly) wary of 'gendered' versions of sin, but acknowledges that sin can be present in different ways, and that for many men and women it is not always shown in overreaching pride. However he argues, from Barth, that incurvature lies behind both pride and sloth. He says, '...sin catapults one into the wrong orbit – oneself – and represents this kind of stultifying, isolating, self-aggrandising *and* self-diminishing posture.' (p186, emphasis original).

Hence the essence of sin is seen to be this incurvature, or at least it is a broad umbrella term for understanding sin. This relates to a more general anthropological point – seeing people as those created for relationship with God and each other. Sin is the act of turning away from such relationships and into ourselves; salvation then causes us to turn outward to love God and neighbour.

There is a direct parallel between Jenson and the work of **Biddle**. Biddle is happy to agree with the traditional conception of sin as pride whereby mankind overreaches in their desire to be 'like God'. In his words we try to become 'more than human'. However he says this is only half the picture. He also argues for sin as an abdication of our place in creation. It is a failure to embrace authentic humanity and in this move we become 'less than human'. We could see both these within the Gen 3 account in that there is the prideful desire to be like God but also the failure to rule over the animals shown in listening to the serpent. These two categories of sin have direct parallels with those of pride and sloth discussed above. As a result of these categories, authentic humanity is seen to require holding onto our creation in God's image *and* our creaturely finitude; that is to live up to God's image, while accepting we're not God. We can fall in two directions.

Within the second category of 'less than human' not all of Biddle's arguments hold water. He makes much of the concept of 'missing the mark' (the title of the book). The Hebrew term for this can be used of literally missing a target and so Biddle argues that this missing is not necessarily deliberate – archers don't intend to miss, rather other factors influence them. Hence he says much sin is failing because of weakness rather than rebelling because of pride. However the verb in question is used of deliberate disobedience in many places (e.g. Gen 39:9) or is commonly paralleled with it (e.g. Josh 7:11). Despite this etymological issue there is something here: Eve was deceived in such a way that she pathetically gave in to a creature rather than exercising dominion over it. Biddle helpfully traces this type of failure through Scripture.

He then argues that these two forms of sin, rebellious pride and failing through weakness, have a common cause behind them. He says: 'the Bible, modern depth psychology … and constructive theology all agree to some extent that underlying both forms of sin, human beings abandon authentic existence out of a sense of anxiety rooted in mistrust' (p75).

This mistrust of God is specifically identified as doubting that God's creation is well-ordered or that he will be faithful and act benevolently towards us. This is related to modern psychological understandings of trust and anxiety.

Biddle's argument here seems to present an inherent instability in creation, such that humanity will fall one of these two ways. He says, 'Humans find it difficult to embrace God's pronouncement that human existence at the boundary between animal and divine is inherently good... Humans overreach to compensate or underattain in despair.' (p75-76). This seems to call into question God's wisdom in how he positioned mankind in the world. Of course any account of sin can be open to this charge – why we sin in the first place is rightly referred to as a mystery. Biddle, however, seems close to suggesting he has solved this mystery: psychological understanding of our difficulties to trust an unseen God make sin almost understandable.

However, Biddle's discussion of the biblical data does give credence to his view of doubt underlying our sin. Genesis 3 clearly turns on the serpent casting doubt on God's word such that God is not trusted. The desert wanderings include accounts of doubting God's goodness; in particular Deut 9:23 suggests that rebellion against God's command to enter the land was because of not believing him. Although not cited by Biddle two keys texts he could have used would be Rom 14:23 ('everything that does not come from faith is sin'), and Heb 11:6 ('without faith it is impossible to please God'). We mentioned earlier that both Calvin and Luther saw unbelief as close to the heart of sin.

So Biddle and Jenson agree on the different ways sin can be expressed – pride (being more than human) or sloth (being less than human). And they agree that there is a fundamental move behind these, the essence of sin. For Jenson it is the gravity of sin where the self turns inward, for Biddle it is mistrust of God. Of course these do not need to be mutually exclusive – one could turn inward because of mistrust – and we'll return to that.

Plantinga approaches his discussion of sin in a very different way. He begins with the biblical idea of 'shalom', the harmony of how God meant things to be. Sin is then whatever wrecks shalom; it is moral vandalism in God's world. Within this big picture view of sin he gives more specific comments on sin being acts and dispositions that displease God and deserve blame. In this sense Plantinga is closer to Campbell in focusing on lawbreaking but he has placed it in a creation setting: 'God hates sin not just because it violates his law but, more substantively, because it violates shalom, because it breaks the peace, because it interferes with the way things are supposed to be' (p14).

Plantinga also gives a much more organic feel to sin than lawbreaking. He does this through a variety of metaphors. So sin is 'corruption', it is like a spiritual virus in God's good creation. Sin results in 'perversion' so we use our energies for wrong ends and purposes. Sin is a 'pollution' which defiles God's good purposes. Within this discussion are many insightful comments and memorable phrases. For example sin is both 'fatal and fertile': it brings death but it also spreads. It is like cancer in that it kills because it reproduces.

Plantinga, like Jenson and Biddle above, recognises that sin can be expressed in different forms. His last two chapters focus on two key forms using the terms of 'fight' or 'flight'. We either attack God in open transgression, attempting to dethrone him, or we run away from him and evade our responsibility. To bring these back to the picture of shalom, he says that 'by the sins of attack we vandalise shalom; by the sins of flight we abandon it' (p197). In this conception there is a clear similarity with Biddle's and Jenson's use of pride and sloth. Plantinga has less discussion of what motivates such moves – his focus is more on how sin infects, corrupts and enslaves us – however he edges towards Biddle's concept of mistrust, speaking of how our knowledge of God should lead to trust and obedience (p196).

Fallen is harder to assess on the essence of sin as it is written by multiple authors. However we can make a few comments. House (on *Sin in the Law*) sees sin as a matter of belief flowing both from our view of God and our desires: 'Humans inevitably choose to believe someone other than God because they want something that God has not promised or because they simply do not believe what God has declared' (p63). The essence of sin then again revolves around who we trust.

Moo's helpful discussion on sin and the law (in his chapter *Sin in Paul*) includes a statement that 'sin can be defined as disobedience to the law' (p113, I can hear Campbell cheering). However he also discusses the essence of sin specifically and draws on Romans 1: sin is relational with regard to God and consists of a refusal to give thanks to him or glorify him. He also says that sin can be seen as lack of faith because everything that does not come from faith is sin (quoting Rom 14:23 which we mentioned earlier).

Mahoney (on *A Theology of Sin for Today*) describes sin as 'both a failure to glorify the Lord and an active rebellion against his established standards' (p194). Hence sin is seen as having both a negative and positive aspect: sin is what is missing in an action that means we fail to glorify God, and it is a trespass and deviation from what God has said. This gets close to Biddle's pictures of failure and pride, but here both are conceived of with regard to breaking the law and later Mahoney states that the 'essence of sin is the violation of a specific command of God' (p215). But again this violation is seen to contain two dimensions: both defiance and disregard of God.

Summary

What is striking from these very different books is the amount of overlap in discussion of the essence of sin (even when that is not the focus of the book). Most of the authors believe that sin can take very different forms, and agree that, in subtly different ways, these can be divided into two. These are presented as pride and sloth, over-reaching and under-reaching, fight and flight, defiance and disregard, self-aggrandising and self-diminishing.

Several authors would remind us of sin as lawbreaking and we've mentioned the clear biblical basis for this. To bring these thoughts together we might say that sin does indeed involve breaking God's law but one can do that in different ways – by rebellious pride, or by pathetic failure – and that both are culpable.

The discussion of the essence of sin often revolves around areas of unbelief or lack of trust in God – again presented with different nuances by different authors. We should be aware here that in biblical terms there is no difference between belief, trust or faith (they are all reasonable translations of the common Greek word in question; it is the English language that gives them different connotations). Whether we believe God's word to us and will trust him is foundational to sin. Doubt leads to disobedience; mistrust to misdeeds.

Jenson's proposal of the image of incurvature doesn't preclude this more basic motivation, and gives a rich picture of the relational outworking of sin which has significant pastoral cash value. In discussing sin we can always ask, 'In what way does this sin show you've turned in on yourself as the centre of the world?' And in encouraging repentance and sanctification we can ask, 'What would turning outward towards God and other people look like here?'

Behind this inward turn though is the dynamic of mistrust/unbelief. We turn inward because we don't believe God. Such a lack of faith and inward turn can then be expressed in different ways, most commonly in wilful arrogance and culpable negligence.

All of this is of great significance in the ways we mentioned earlier. It helps us see the *unity* of sin, within the variety of presentations and narratives Scripture gives us. We can ask, 'In what way does this picture of sin, or example of sin, show a lack of trust in God, or unbelief in his word?' That is not to push us to flatten out the rich biblical portrait of sin but to aid us in consistency of teaching. Within pastoral counselling we can ask, 'In what way is this person not trusting God's word to them?' Or, 'What truth about God do they need to believe?' And we will see that this is the essential dynamic behind presentations of sin which at first glance look very different, from the obviously angry and rebellious, to the apathetic and self-pitying.

We will also be better able to *apply* the doctrine of sin to a variety of people. If sin flows from not trusting God then it will show itself in many middle class, respectable sins, just as much as in the more obviously 'lawbreaking' sins. For many people it is probably the sin as sloth, the abandonment of who we are as those made in God's image, that leads to the less obvious sins of negligence shown by those who might otherwise appear very pleasant. In our teaching and pastoring we will then be more able to show everyone that they are a sinner, even if they look different to those they regard as 'sinners'. More than that we will be able to show them that their sin grows from the same root. Indeed, at root they are no different. Our doctrine of sin should be one of the most humbling and levelling truths we teach, and this will help it be so.

And lastly we will be able to *help* people more in sanctification. This shows us that the fight against sin is the fight to trust God. As John Owen argued, we will only defeat indwelling sin by faith. This quickly leads to the importance of our picture of God as the one who can be trusted. The fight against sin is closely linked to the fight for a clear picture of the gloriously good and faithful God that I can commit myself to.

The importance of this can be seen in Sinclair Ferguson's recent book *The Whole Christ* (Crossway, 2016). Ferguson argues that two common problems in sanctification – antinomianism and legalism – actually have the same root cause: a lack of trust in God. The answer to each of these is not a dose of the other, for that would only be to disbelieve God in a different way. Rather we must help people gain a picture of God as the one they can and should trust fully. Such pastoral wisdom flows from understanding the essence of sin. P

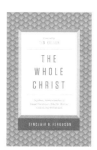

Sin

"...lives off the good, yet fights it to the point of destruction.

It is nothing, has nothing, and cannot do anything without the entities and forces God has created, yet organises all into rebellion against him.

With everything that belongs to God, it opposes everything that belongs to God.

It is the will of a weak, finite creature in its revolt against the Creator.

It is dependence at war with the Independent One and striving for its own independence.

It is impermanent becoming in a struggle with him who exists eternally.

It is the greatest contradiction tolerated by God in his creation, yet used by him in the way of justice and righteousness as an instrument for his glory."

Herman Bavinck
Reformed Dogmatics, Vol. 3: Sin and Salvation in Christ
ed. John Bolt (Grand Rapids: Baker Academic, 2003)

THE HERALD

BAD NEWS

Tim Ward reflects on how we preach sin to unbelievers and believers

PREACHING SIN EVANGELISTICALLY

"Sin is first of all a *condition* that is simultaneously judicial and moral, legal and relational." So says the theologian Michael Horton, helpfully pointing out some of the breadth of the Bible's presentation of sin. In recent times the two poles which Horton's definition covers have sometimes been pitted against each other as opposing views which

Michael Horton, *The Christian Faith: A Systematic Theology for Pilgrims on the Way* (Grand Rapids: Zondervan, 2011), 427.

we must choose between, in terms of presenting sin as *rebellion* and sin as *idolatry*. Preaching sin as rebellion is to work within judicial and legal categories; preaching sin as idolatry is to engage on more moral and relational grounds. Both presentations of sin of course have a long pedigree in orthodox Christian preaching.

Evangelicals are usually (and rightly!) people committed to evangelism as a high priority, and it is therefore not a great surprise that our theology sometimes emerges just as much as a reflection on the kind of evangelistic preaching that we think it makes sense to engage in, as it provides the basis on which we build our evangelistic preaching.

In popular evangelism, the best known example of 'sin as rebellion' is perhaps the gospel-training tool *Two Ways To Live*, which in the second of its six simple pictures portrays sin as a rebellion against God as the rightful king, with God represented by a large crown and sin by a little crown with which humanity tries to crown itself. The operative word at this point in the text that accompanies this short gospel-explanation is "rule". I reckon that quite a high proportion of conservative evangelical preachers (I may be one of them!) default regularly to describing sin as rebellion. I also reckon that we do so in large part because as younger Christians our training in evangelism was heavily influenced by *Two Ways To Live*. It is a view of sin that thinks of God primarily as a kingly rule-maker and of humanity as his rule-breaking subjects.

By contrast, there has been a growing stream of evangelistic preaching that prefers to default to preaching sin in terms of idolatry. One particular source of influence here that many would be aware of is Tim Keller's writing and preaching. This is a view of sin which thinks of God primarily as a divine being to whom our worship is due, and of humanity as naturally worshipping creatures who misdirect their worship to created things rather than to the creator. Some corners of conservative evangelicalism are suspicious of such a strong focus on 'sin as idolatry.' I think this is so not primarily because they always have clearly biblical objections but because they have misgivings about wider elements of Keller's vision for and practice of mission, and fear that a strong focus on preaching sin as idolatry inevitably feeds into such things. These missiological matters are not my concern here, although it's important to point out that it is possible to think it right to have a very strong focus on idolatry in one's preaching on sin without necessarily buying in to any particular person's wider viewpoint on other matters.

Illustration from *Two Ways to Live* © Matthias Media. Used with permission. See *twowaystolive.com* for more information.

I suggest that some are also worried about a strong idolatry-focus in preaching sin because it seems to them that it risks downplaying the seriousness of sin, at least in contrast with a rebellion-focus. After all, in identifying sin as idolatry something positive is actually being said about humanity in sin: that we worship. The fault being identified is fundamentally one of misdirection or misalignment of a God-given characteristic, and it can feel as if this is rather further away from a strong sense of the utter seriousness of sin than a proclamation that the hearers are simply rebels. In a moment I will explore this briefly within Genesis 3. For now, however, it needs to be noted that assertions of the centrality of idolatry to our doctrine of sin can be found in writing far wider than those concerned with contemporary evangelistic or missiological categories. For example, Garry Williams has recently stated in a theological work on the love of God: "The Bible is clear that idolatry is at the heart of sin. That is not to say that sin is only to be understood as idolatry - there are other essential aspects in any definition of sin - but sin is always at least idolatry."

Garry J. Williams, *His Love Endures For Ever: Reflections on the Love of God* (Nottingham: IVP, 2015), 60.

Painting with a broad brush, I would contend that strong proponents of either 'sin as rebellion' or 'sin as idolatry' are each partly driven by strong but somewhat different evangelistic convictions. Preaching sin as idolatry lends itself, as already noted, to identifying something positive in fallen humanity (the desire to worship); it invites the preacher to explore features of contemporary culture in depth in order to expose them as modern-day idols. In other words, it offers an invitingly fruitful understanding of sin for preachers who are keen to be heard to engage strongly with contemporary culture, and to do so positively as well as negatively. There is of course of good biblical and historical warrant for doing both of those things, to some degree, in evangelistic preaching (Paul in Athens, Acts 17, is an obvious example).

By contrast, the preaching of sin as rebellion tends to work itself out in a more obviously negative understanding of humanity and of culture, since it focuses on identifying those areas of life and culture in which we live in flat-out disobedience to God. My observation is that this way of preaching sin appeals strongly to preachers who worry that a concern to engage with the specifics of culture, and to be heard to speak quite positively as well as negatively about unregenerate life, is sowing the seeds for a significant downplaying of sin. They worry, further, that this in turn usually leads to a lessening of the wonder of God's act of salvation in Christ. And again there is of course plenty of good biblical and historical warrant for portraying life outside Christ in such terms.

At the risk of sounding a little abstract, an observation on the nature of Christian doctrine should help here. When a question arises such as the one I've been addressing - is sin in Scripture primarily to do with idolatry or primarily to do with rebellion? - it may well be that the very form of the question implies a wrong assumption about

Christian doctrine, namely, that every properly constructed biblical doctrine has one particular concept that is 'primary,' being at its core or its heart, and all other related concepts are not quite as central and somehow flow from that core or heart. God, however, has caused Scripture to be written for us in a form and with a richness which suggests that often, within any particular doctrine, there are a variety of perspectives and images and concepts which are all vital, interrelated and in various ways 'central,' with each needing to be preached with a sensitivity to the others in a way that reflects the biblical emphases and relations between them. These emphases and relations can only be discerned through the most careful exegetical and biblical-theological work.

One small piece of evidence that something like this is the case with the different aspects of the doctrine of sin can be found in the first part of Genesis 3, which at the very least is a pretty fundamental chapter in Scripture for our understanding of sin.

GOD, HOWEVER, HAS CAUSED SCRIPTURE TO BE WRITTEN FOR US IN A FORM AND WITH A RICHNESS WHICH SUGGESTS THAT OFTEN, WITHIN ANY PARTICULAR DOCTRINE, THERE ARE A VARIETY OF PERSPECTIVES AND IMAGES AND CONCEPTS WHICH ARE ALL VITAL, INTERRELATED AND IN VARIOUS WAYS 'CENTRAL,' WITH EACH NEEDING TO BE PREACHED WITH A SENSITIVITY TO THE OTHERS IN A WAY THAT REFLECTS THE BIBLICAL EMPHASES AND RELATIONS BETWEEN THEM.

Genesis 3:1-7

¹Now the snake was more crafty than any of the wild animals the Lord God had made. He said to the woman, 'Did God really say, "You must not eat from any tree in the garden"?'

²The woman said to the snake, 'We may eat fruit from the trees in the garden, ³but God did say, "You must not eat fruit from the tree that is in the middle of the garden, and you must not touch it, or you will die."'

⁴'You will not certainly die,' the snake said to the woman. ⁵'For God knows that when you eat from it your eyes will be opened, and you will be like God, knowing good and evil.'

⁶When the woman saw that the fruit of the tree was good for food and pleasing to the eye, and also desirable for gaining wisdom, she took some and ate it. She also gave some to her husband, who was with her, and he ate it. ⁷Then the eyes of both of them were opened, and they realised that they were naked; so they sewed fig leaves together and made coverings for themselves.

A few observations are worth making from this chapter. None of them is particularly original, but it's helpful to grasp a little of the complexity of the nature of sin as presented even in this short and early section of Scripture:

➦ Satanically caused confusion about the nature of what God has actually said is presented as central in what causes humanity to sin (3:1-3).

➦ This builds up to a flat-out denial by Satan of the truth of the threat God has made about what will happen if humanity disobeys him (3:4), and the effect this has on Eve is also presented as central in what causes humanity to sin.

➦ The further temptation that the serpent offers is subtle: "For God knows that when you eat from it your eyes will be opened, and you will be like God, knowing good and evil" (3:5). There's no space here to discuss the precise meaning of each of these phrases, but what is clear is that Satan has shifted from stating an outright lie (3:4) to offering a tempting half-truth. Something that it is not proper for humanity to seek after (being "like God, knowing good and evil") is dangled in front of Eve as something good for her to pursue, but Satan presents it in terms which are not entirely false. An urge within humanity to be in some senses "like God" is good and right, if pursued to the right ends and by the right means (e.g. ruling as he rules, under him, Gen. 1:26-28). I think it can rightly be said that the subtle temptation offered here by the serpent to Eve in just a few words is both a temptation to rebel against God as law-giver ("be like me in these ways..., but unlike me in these ways..."), and also a temptation to misdirect a God-given aspect of humanity in its createdness. It would be difficult to argue from this text that one is more predominant than the other; both are present, and inextricably linked.

➡ That feature continues in the next verse, 3:6: "When the woman saw that the fruit of the tree was good for food and pleasing to the eye, and also desirable for gaining wisdom, she took some and ate it." The final words in that sentence about Eve taking and eating implicitly portray her actions as straight-out rebellious disobedience to divine instruction, echoing as they do the command of God in 2:17 ("but you must not eat from the tree of the knowledge of good and evil").

➡ However the first part of 3:6, which gives (for Scripture) unusually explicit insight into a character's mind, speaks less of rebellion and more about misdirection of fundamentally good desires. To nourish oneself on fruit that looks appetising ("good for food") can be a thoroughly good thing to do, in light of God's words in 1:29 about his provision of food. To act in response to that which is aesthetically pleasing ("pleasing to the eye") can be a thoroughly good thing to do, in light of God's own judgment that each element of creation is good and that its completed totality is "very good" (1:31). And to want to profit from something that will give wisdom ("desirable for gaining wisdom") can likewise be a good thing, in light of the task of dominion which God has entrusted to humanity (1:28). It would not be right, of course, to find idolatry expressed directly in this, but the bad seed which will later flower into that ugly plant is present: a sinful misdirection of essentially virtuous characteristics and instincts.

The two basic categories on which the differing notions of 'sin as rebellion' and 'sin as idolatry' are built can both be found then, I suggest, strongly interwoven in this, the earliest biblical passage on sin. Is there a good perspective within which they can both be held together? Although not all might think it right to use such language with regard to Genesis 3, for myself the best candidate for a very 'bottom-level' description of sin as it is revealed to us here is to see it as covenant-breaking. Covenant is a rich concept (and highly disputed, of course!), and has the great virtue of holding together in integral unity the notions which support each of the two models for presenting sin that I have been discussing: God is a being worthy of worship, and sin is misdirection of that worship; God is a regal law-giver, and sin is rebellion against his rule.

PREACHING SIN TO BELIEVERS

I now want to turn to the way in which we are to preach sin to those who are already believers in Jesus Christ. In particular I have in mind what preachers say to believers about our own ongoing sin.

Here is what I am going to propose:

I observe that it is very common for evangelical preachers to default to speaking regularly of believers as 'sinners'. I mean something specific here: we tend to speak not only (as we must) of believers as people who continue to commit and struggle against sin; we also regularly go further and speak not only of believers as people who do sinful things but also categorise believers under the personal description 'sinner'. We of course gloriously add to that '*forgiven* sinner' or 'sinner *saved by grace*', but nevertheless the noun 'sinner' is still taken to apply to the believer, as something further to the verb 'sinning'. My proposal is that conservative evangelical preachers often make this category-description of believers, and do so rather more regularly than the NT does.

This needs some substantiation from Scripture, and I'll introduce two passages. By any reckoning, Romans 6 is a significant part of Scripture that deals directly with the question of the relationship between the believer and sin. I'll focus on Rom 6:6-7: "For we know that our old self was crucified with him so that the body ruled by sin might be done away with, that we should

Although strictly speaking not quite so straight-forwardly, since the Greek verb translated 'set free' in Rom 6:7 by NIV and ESV is actually *dikaioo*, which is often translated 'justify' (see ESV footnote). Most commentators agree that NIV and ESV (main text) have rightly translated the sense.

no longer be slaves to sin - because anyone who has died has been set free from sin."

That final clause asserts very straightforwardly that believers have been "set free" from sin, because that is the state of anyone who has died, and in 6:6 Paul has just categorised believers among those who have indeed died (specifically, by virtue of our old self having been crucified with Christ). I suspect that if we said to those who regularly hear our preaching, "Put up your hand if you've been set free from sin," hardly a soul would dare to do so - and any who did might do so for entirely wrong theological reasons, rather than because they've understood and believed Romans 6. If I'm right about this (and if you reckon your church family would be a glorious exception to my general rule, do forgive me), I suggest that this reveals something that's not quite biblically right about our default way of speaking of believers and their sin.

What's sometimes missing in our preaching about sin is the background of Paul's teaching about our having been crucified with Christ and having been raised with Christ. These are very black-and-white categories that refer to personal identity. Either you have died with Christ or you have not. Either you have been raised with Christ or you are still dead in your sins. In Romans 6 Paul teaches these realities about the believer in order to make his primary point about the fundamental break that has occurred between the believer and sin. Because that background teaching about Christ and the believer does not always figure

WHAT'S SOMETIMES MISSING IN OUR PREACHING ABOUT SIN IS THE BACKGROUND OF PAUL'S TEACHING ABOUT OUR HAVING BEEN CRUCIFIED WITH CHRIST AND HAVING BEEN RAISED WITH CHRIST.

as prominently in evangelical preaching as it should, we do not often make the consequently radical point about sin and the believer that Paul does.

Our most commonly used language to describe the breach in the believer's relationship with sin which has already occurred is, I suggest, language of forgiveness. The only complete 'already' for the believer with regard to sin is often assumed to be freedom and acquittal from the legal consequence of condemnation for sin. Paul however, in Romans 6, has rather more to say than that about the already existing breach between the believer and sin. When Paul does go on to speak in Romans 6 about ongoing sin in the believer he pointedly switches from setting believers in one *category* or another to speaking of *actions* which relate to sin: sin exercising a reign in us, and us offering parts of ourselves to sin (6:12-13).

A similar theme can be found in the first part of 2 Peter. More than one sermon I've heard (and, I willingly confess, have preached myself) on 2 Pet 1:1-11 has highlighted 1:8: "For if you possess these qualities

in increasing measure, they will keep you from being ineffective and unproductive in your knowledge of our Lord Jesus Christ." The preacher goes on something like this: "You don't want to be a Christian who only produces a *little* fruit, do you? You want to be a Christian who is *really* effective for the Lord, don't you? Well then, you've got to strive to grow in all the qualities listed in 1:5-7." If that sounds at all familiar as a basic exegetical and homiletical approach to this text, just note what's going on here. First, the assumption is being made that the passage is essentially dealing with the question of a sliding-scale of Christian virtues, as if its primary theme were to do with encouragement to demonstrate rather more of this and that in order to be rather more productive and effective as a believer. Second, note the pastoral effect of this. In order to have a punchy application, the preacher taking this approach will normally look for hard-hitting applications which will make even the most productive and effective believer present, if they have a soft heart, feel rebuked by their failure to grow yet further in one or other of the listed virtues.

I want to suggest that this 'sliding-scale of virtues/effectiveness' interpretation of passages such as 2 Pet 1:1-11 comes very naturally to many evangelical preachers. It is not, however, quite correct with regard to this text. Instead, the basic categories which Peter is dealing with are rather more like Paul's 'black and white' categories of Romans 6:6-7. See 2 Pet 1:4: believers are those who "hav[e] escaped the corruption in the world caused by evil desires." The 'already' of our breach with sin, as with Romans 6, extends further than freedom from condemnation; it extends to actual corruption in the world. (As before, I wonder how many people of good conscience in our churches would say of themselves, "Yes I have indeed escaped the corruption in the world causes by evil desires.")

Look also at the end of the section. Verse 10 speaks of doing 'these things' ("For if you do these things, you will never stumble.") And "these things" seem in context to be the virtues and practices listed in 1:5-7. That also suggests that the command to "make every effort to confirm your calling and election" is not something different from what has come previously, but is a different (and more serious) perspective from which Peter repeats essentially the same command as in 1:5 ("make every effort..."). In other words, there is really no sliding-scale at work in this passage along the lines of "make sure you're more rather than less effective as a Christian." What is fundamentally at work here is a pair of either/or categories: believers are defined as those who know the Lord Jesus and do so effectively and productively,

In the wider context of this letter Peter will turn out to have especially in mind here those scoffers who seem to claim to be Christian teachers but who deny the future glorious coming of Christ in judgment, whose error produces no fruit of godliness in their own lives or in the lives of those who listen to them (2:1-3).

and unbelievers are defined as those who don't. This is confirmed, I suggest, by the straightforward either/or eschatological categories that control 1:10b-11, with which the section concludes: those who stumble (not by sinning a bit more than others, but by failing to reach heaven), are contrasted with those who are welcomed into Christ's kingdom (the point of the "rich" welcome here being not to do with more fulsome and less fulsome kinds of welcome into the kingdom, but that there's only one kind of welcome on offer, and it's a rich one.)

If a preacher sees this fundamental theme running through the passage, his application to believers is rather less likely to slide into a flattened-out exhortation to all to live out 1:5-7 more effectively, pointing out areas in which everyone's failing. He may at times touch on that, but it is not likely to be central. Instead he will carefully distinguish between "knowledge of Jesus Christ" which does not produce any fruit or effectiveness at all, such as is described later in the letter in the 'scoffers', and therefore leads certainly to final stumbling and exclusion from the kingdom, and the fruit that is being produced effectively among believers because those believers are heeding the command of 1:5-7.

Some concluding remarks, bringing together the conclusions from these brief treatments of Romans 6 and 2 Peter 1:

There are of course passages in Scripture whose primary purpose is to urge all believers to fight even harder against sin that remains.

That is not in dispute. Ephesians 4:17ff. is a good example. What I am observing is that such passages don't often speak of believers in the category of 'sinner', while still speaking strongly of the acts of sin which believers are to mortify.

The NT speaks rather more often than evangelical preaching sometimes does of absolute categories with regard to sin, with the believer put firmly already on the opposite side to sin. Romans 6 does so in terms of already having been freed from sin; 2 Peter 1 does so in terms of having already escaped the corruption in the world. Preaching on such texts can easily slide into presenting different categories - sliding-scale ones of 'a bit more sinful/a bit less sinful' - in order to cash out with an application of moral exhortation to believers.

The most unfortunate consequence of this tendency, where it exists, is that believers' assurance is often wrongly, although usually unwittingly, undermined. The glorious 'already' aspects of the breach that God has brought about in our relationship with sin are shaved off, and all that's left are its legal aspects. I've suggested that an underplaying of the either/or NT realities of dying and rising with Christ often sits in the background of this.

There are a number of books which highlight this central theme of the union of the believer with Christ. Here are a few, starting with the lightest at the top, and getting meatier as you work down:

Rory Shiner, *One Forever: The Transforming Power of Being in Christ* (Kingsford NSW: Matthias Media, 2012)

Steve Timmis & Christopher de la Hoyde, *In Christ: In Him Together for the World* (Ross-shire: Christian Focus, 2014)

Marcus Peter Johnson, *One With Christ: An Evangelical Theology of Salvation* (Wheaton: Crossway, 2013)

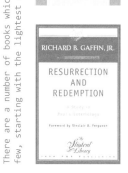

Richard B. Gaffin, Jr., *Resurrection and Redemption: A Study in Paul's Soteriology* (Phillipsburg: Presbyterian & Reformed, 1987)

Simul iustus et peccator ('at the same time justified and sinner') is a terrific, venerable statement of the grace of justification. However that final noun, 'sinner', is not a particularly sharp way of expressing the NT's understanding of the believer's relationship to ongoing sin. The problem, as regards our understanding of sin, is with the noun *peccator* ('sinner') as a label to give directly to the Christian. If we were to tweak the phrase in order to give it value for a doctrine of sin, one possibility might be *simul iustus et peccans* ('at the same time justified and sinning'). We commit sins - yes of course. But gloriously, according to Scripture, we stand not in the category of sinners - in Adam, ruled by sin and death - but in the category of those who by faith are in Christ, who have been given life, even though we were dead. P

An excerpt from John Calvin's *The Institutes of the Christian Religion* with an introduction and annotations by Mark Troughton.

only damnable things come forth from man's corrupt nature

John Calvin at 53 years old in an engraving by René Boyvin

The names Luther, Calvin and Zwingli conjure up different images in our minds; ones that are perhaps more influenced by caricature than actual fact. Indeed, some of Calvin's own students would sketch the great man rather less than flatteringly – his gaunt, wizened, scrawny face with goatee beard, his bony fingers protruding from his heavy fur-collared gown – doubtless out of inverted respect for the theological genius that he was, as he delivered his Bible lectures from St Peter's in Geneva from 1536 onwards.

Appearances and caricatures are, however, in the end, misleading and it would be to our loss if we discarded the wealth of biblical insight that Calvin offers us, particularly in his piercingly accurate diagnosis of the human condition, on the basis of inaccurate caricature. So don't be put off by terms such as 'total depravity'; or allow personal misconceptions about 'Calvinism' or 'Calvinists' to deter you from learning from him; allow Calvin to unpack the biblical worldview for us. Only then, having understood the seriousness of our disease, will we see why the remedy that God provides is so necessary.

In his magnum opus *The Institutes of the Christian Religion*, John Calvin begins with the knowledge of God the Creator, because unless we know him as he truly is, we cannot possibly know ourselves as we truly are (Book 1). Calvin then presents, in Book 2, the knowledge of God the Redeemer by looking firstly at the knowledge of sin (*harmatiology*, to give its technical name). Why? Because unless we realize how sick we really are, we will never be ready to accept the cure that God prescribes for us.

Man by nature inclines to deluded self-admiration; the self-knowledge required is one that strips us of all confidence in our own ability ... In giving man credit for excellence we enhance our innate blind self-love; even if we concede part to God we leave enough to occasion boasting and overconfidence ... In nearly every age, men who have extolled human virtues have been popular because they appeal to men's pride. But those confident they can do anything by their own power hurtle, through self-ignorance, to ruin. (II.1.2)

In Calvin's *Institutes* these numbers refer to the book, chapter and section. So here it's book 2, chapter 1, section 2.

Calvin often rebukes this natural tendency to an overweening self-confidence by referring to human beings as a 5ft worm or worse – unfit to be ranked with worms, lice, fleas and vermin. No wonder he has had his detractors and critics! Though by no means a misanthropist (i.e. a hater of men), Calvin certainly entertained no illusions about the innocence of post-fall humanity. His understanding of Scripture could lead him to no other conclusion.

Calvin proceeds in II.1.4-5 to show how the fall into sin affected every part of humankind, such that no part of us remains without taint since the original sin of our first parents. Humanity's whole being, including our understanding and our will, is now so corrupted as to leave us incapable of self-salvation (what's known as 'total depravity' or inability). Humanity has now been deprived of freedom of choice and bound over to miserable slavery, II.2.1ff.

Chapter 3 of Book II brings Calvin's treatment of sin to its climax by showing how Scripture justifies such a pessimistic view of human nature and so leads us to dependence on God's grace.

We'll be looking at the first six sections in which Calvin covers two issues:

1. *What does Scripture affirm about the corruption of mankind (sections 1-2) and how the obvious objection, 'What about all the good people out there?' can be answered in the section on the virtues of the unconverted (sections 3-4).*

2. *How, as slaves of sin, people must be spiritually regenerated, (5-6).*

If you were to keep reading in the *Institutes* beyond our extract, sections 7-12 develop this thesis further and answer several objections to do with the nature of cooperation in conversion. In the final part of the chapter, Calvin demonstrates how this teaching that all is of God's grace concurs with St Augustine's understanding of man in sin and salvation and that therefore it is nothing new (13-14).

The following excerpt comes from the best available English translation: John T.McNeill, ed. *Calvin: Institutes of the Christian Religion,* translated by Ford Lewis Battles, (Philadelphia: Westminster, 1960). Used with permission from Westminster John Knox Press.

1. The whole man is flesh

But man cannot be better known in both faculties of his soul than if he makes his appearance with those titles whereby Scripture marks him. If the whole man is depicted by these words of Christ, "What is born of flesh, is flesh" [John 3:6] (as is easy to prove), man is very clearly shown to be a miserable creature. "For to set the mind on the flesh," as the apostle testifies, "is death. Because there is enmity against God, it does not submit to God's law, indeed it cannot." [Rom. 8:6-7 p.] Is the flesh so perverse that it is wholly disposed to bear a grudge against God, cannot agree with the justice of divine law, can, in short, beget nothing but the occasion of death? Now suppose that in man's nature there is nothing but flesh: extract something good from it if you can.

But, you will say, the word "flesh" pertains only to the sensual part of the soul, not to the higher part. This is thoroughly refuted from the words of Christ and of the apostle. The Lord's reasoning is: Man must be reborn [John 3:3], for he "is flesh" [John 3:6]. He is not teaching a rebirth as regards the body. Now the soul is not reborn if merely a part of it is reformed, but only when it is wholly renewed. The antithesis set forth in both passages confirms this. The Spirit is so contrasted with flesh that no intermediate thing is left. Accordingly, whatever is not spiritual in man is by this reckoning called "carnal." We have nothing of the Spirit, however, except through regeneration. Whatever we have from nature, therefore, is flesh.

But Paul relieves us of any possible doubt on this matter. Having described the old man who, he had said, was "corrupted by deceptive desires" [Eph. 4:22], he bids us "be renewed in the spirit of our mind" [Eph. 4:23], You see that he lodges unlawful and wicked desires not solely in the sensual part of the soul, but even in the mind itself, and for this reason he requires its renewal. To be sure, a little while before he had painted a picture of human nature that showed us corrupt and perverted in every part. He writes that "all the Gentiles walk in the vanity of their minds, being darkened in their understanding, alienated from the life of God, because of the ignorance which is in them, and their blindness of heart." [Eph. 4:17-18.] There is not the least doubt that this statement applies to all those whom the Lord has not yet formed again to the uprightness of his wisdom and justice.

Our *mind* and *will*, that is.

Calvin's use of 'Flesh' and 'Spirit' are typical of the sharp contrasts found in Paul and John, an attention-grabbing style of writing typical of Jewish Wisdom literature (see Psalm 1).

Paul is countering the common assumption that regards people as bi-partite creatures of flesh (the lower, sensual nature) and spirit (the higher, nobler faculties like reason) and that thinks we can exert mind over matter to improve ourselves. The heresy of Gnosticism will develop this further in the 2nd Century. Calvin, like Jesus and Paul, cuts through this by stating that apart from the Spirit of God we are simply fleshly, ruled by our sinful natures and unable to please God.

This also becomes clearer from the comparison immediately added wherein he admonishes believers that they "did not so learn Christ" [Eph. 4:20]. We, indeed, infer from these words that the grace of Christ is the sole remedy to free us from that blindness and from the evils consequent upon it. Isaiah also had so prophesied concerning Christ's Kingdom when he promised: "The Lord will be an everlasting light" for his church [Isa. 60:19], while "shadows will shroud the earth and darkness will cover the peoples" [ch. 60:2]. He there testifies that the light of God will arise in the church alone; and leaves only shadows and blindness outside the church.

I shall not individually recount the statements made everywhere concerning men's vanity, especially in the Psalms and the Prophets. Great is the utterance of David: "Those of low estate are but a breath; those of high estate are a delusion; in the balances they go up; they are together lighter than a breath" (NIV). Man's understanding is pierced by a heavy spear when all the thoughts that proceed from him are mocked as stupid, frivolous, insane, and perverse.

2. Romans ch. 3 as witness for man's corruption

That condemnation of the heart when it is called "deceitful and corrupt above all else" [Jer. 17:9] is no less severe. But because I am striving for brevity, I shall be content with but one passage; yet it will be like the clearest of mirrors in which we may contemplate the whole image of our nature. For the apostle, when he wishes to cast down the arrogance of humankind, does so by these testimonies: 'No one is righteous, no one understands, no one seeks God. All have turned aside, together they have become unprofitable; no one does good, not even one' [Ps. 14:1-3; 53:1-3]. 'Their throat is an open grave, they use their tongues deceitfully' [Ps. 5:9]. 'The venom of asps is under their lips' [Ps. 140:3]. 'Their mouth is full of cursing and bitterness' [Ps. 10:7]. 'Their feet are swift to shed blood; in their paths are ruin and misery' [Isa. 59:7]. 'There is no fear of God before their eyes' [Rom. 3:10-16, 18].

With these thunderbolts he inveighs not against particular men but against the whole race of Adam's

Calvin is about to answer the quite natural objection, "But I know some really nice non-Christians, surely this is overstating it?"

children. Nor is he decrying the depraved morals of one age or another, but indicting the unvarying corruption of our nature. Now his intention in this passage is not simply to rebuke men that they may repent, but rather to teach them that they have all been overwhelmed by an unavoidable calamity from which only God's mercy can deliver them. Because this could not be proved unless it rested upon the ruin and destruction of our nature, he put forward these testimonies which prove our nature utterly lost.

Let this then be agreed: that men are as they are here described not merely by the defect of depraved custom, but also by depravity of nature. The reasoning of the apostle cannot otherwise stand: Except out of the Lord's mercy there is no salvation for man, for in himself he is lost and forsaken [Rom. 3:23 ff.]. I shall not toil in proving the applicability of these passages, in order that they may not seem to have been inappropriately seized upon by the apostle. I shall proceed as if these statements had first been made by Paul, not drawn from the Prophets.

First of all, he strips man of righteousness, that is, integrity and purity; then, of understanding [Rom. 3:10-11]. Indeed, apostasy from God proves defect of understanding, for to seek him is the first degree of wisdom. This defect, therefore, is necessarily found in all who have forsaken God. He adds that all have fallen away and have, as it were, become corrupt, that there is no one who does good.

Then he adds the shameful acts with which they – once they have been let loose in wickedness – defile their several members.

Finally, he declares them devoid of the fear of God, to whose rule our steps ought to have been directed. If these are the hereditary endowments of the human race, it is futile to seek anything good in our nature; yet one cannot deny that this hydra lurks in the breast of each. For as the body, so long as it nourishes in itself the cause and matter of disease (even though pain does not yet rage), will not be called healthy, so also will the soul not be considered healthy while it abounds with so many fevers of vice. This comparison, however, does not fit in every detail. For in the diseased body some vigor of life yet remains; although the soul, plunged into this deadly abyss, is not only burdened with vices, but is utterly devoid of all good.

Calvin's intention, like Paul's, is not to stand self-righteously above other people, but to reveal the seriousness of the disease of sin so that people realise their need of a cure.

That is, sin is not merely the result of socio-economic factors such as bad housing, poor upbringing and education or material poverty, but is something that is genetically transmitted from generation to generation, and which affects every sector of society, regardless of privilege.

Calvin takes it for granted that these verses cited from the Old Testament were just as true of Paul's day in the 1st century as of the Psalmists'. Likewise, there were more than sufficient examples of the type of sinful behaviour the Psalms describe in the France of the 16th century not to warrant going any further. Has anything changed today? Not if you read the newspaper or watch the TV news.

Calvin is referring here to the labours of Hercules from Greek Mythology: each time he cut off one head of the hydra it would grow another in its place. Likewise sins of all sorts lurk within the human heart, awaiting their opportunity to grow.

3. God's grace sometimes restrains where it does not cleanse

Almost the same question that was previously answered now confronts us anew. In every age there have been persons who, guided by nature, have striven toward virtue throughout life. I have nothing to say against them even if many lapses can be noted in their moral conduct. For they have by the very zeal of their honesty given proof that there was some purity in their nature.

Although in discussing merit of works we shall deal more fully with what value such virtues have in God's sight, we must nevertheless speak of it also at this point, inasmuch as it is necessary for the unfolding of the present argument. These examples, accordingly, seem to warn us against adjudging man's nature wholly corrupted, because some men have by its prompting not only excelled in remarkable deeds, but conducted themselves most honorably throughout life. But here it ought to occur to us that amid this corruption of nature there is some place for God's grace; not such grace as to cleanse it, but to restrain it inwardly. For if the Lord gave loose rein to the mind of each man to run riot in his lusts, there would doubtless be no one who would not show that, in fact, every evil thing for which Paul condemns all nature is most truly to be met in himself [Ps. 14:3; Rom. 3:12].

What then? Do you count yourself exempt from the number of those whose "feet are swift to shed blood" [Rom. 3:15], whose hands are fouled with robberies and murders, "whose throats are like open graves, whose tongues deceive, whose lips are envenomed" [Rom. 3:13]; whose works are useless, wicked, rotten, deadly; whose hearts are without God; whose inmost parts, depravities; whose eyes are set upon stratagems; whose minds are eager to revile – to sum up, whose every part stands ready to commit infinite wickedness [Rom. 3:10-18]?

If every soul is subject to such abominations as the apostle boldly declares, we surely see what would happen if the Lord were to permit human lust to wander

This is so helpful because in our own experience we know that we are not allowed to become as bad as we might possibly be, owing to such restraining influences exerted upon us as upbringing, education, conscience, good role models, the forces of law and order, etc. All of these Calvin attributes to God's common grace (to be distinguished from his special grace in conversion).

according to its own inclination. No mad beast would rage as unrestrainedly; no river, however swift and violent, burst so madly into flood. In his elect the Lord cures these diseases in a way that we shall soon explain. Others he merely restrains by throwing a bridle over them only that they may not break loose, inasmuch as he foresees their control to be expedient to preserve all that is. Hence some are restrained by shame from breaking out into many kinds of foulness, others by the fear of the law – even though they do not, for the most part, hide their impurity. Still others, because they consider an honest manner of life profitable, in some measure aspire to it. Others rise above the common lot, in order by their excellence to keep the rest obedient to them. Thus God by his providence bridles perversity of nature, that it may not break forth into action; but he does not purge it within.

4. Uprightness is God's gift; but man's nature remains corrupted

Nevertheless the problem has not yet been resolved. For either we must make Camillus equal to Catiline, or we shall have in Camillus an example proving that nature, if carefully cultivated, is not utterly devoid of goodness. Indeed, I admit that the endowments resplendent in Camillus were gifts of God and seem rightly commendable if judged in themselves. But how will these serve as proofs of natural goodness in him? Must we not hark back to his mind and reason thus: if a natural man excelled in such moral integrity, undoubtedly human nature did not lack the ability to cultivate virtue? Yet what if the mind had been wicked and crooked, and had followed anything but uprightness? And there is no doubt that it was such, if you grant that Camillus was a natural man. What power for good will you attribute to human nature in this respect, if in the loftiest appearance of integrity, it is always found to be impelled toward corruption? Therefore as you will not commend a man for virtue when his vices impress you under the appearance of virtues, so you will not attribute to the human will the capability of seeking after the right so long as the will remains set in its own perversity.

Not in the unconverted; in the converted He uses all kinds of ways to purify us in order that we might share in His holiness, Hebrews 12.10.

For Christians, sanctification is both positional (definitive) at conversion and progressive through life, 1 Thess 5.23; 1 John 3.2-3.

1 Cor 1.2 shows how the believers in Corinth were both positionally holy (set apart at conversion to belong to God - 'sanctified') and yet were being made holy progressively ('and called to be holy') through such means as, for example, the Apostle Paul's exhortations to holiness, 1 Cor 1.10; 5.1; 6.1.

Camillus (circa 400BC) was a Roman famous for his high morals, whereas Catiline, a 1st century Roman senator, was roundly rebuked by Cicero for his conspiratorial treachery and low morals.

Calvin is addressing the issue of how it is that sinful people can do good. The possible answers are a) good and evil do not really exist ('making Camillus equal to Catiline') b) people are not 'totally depraved', witness Camillus, a good man. c) Calvin's view: no matter how much good we see in somebody, no one is flawless. But the good that we do see is a gift of God (common grace). The sin is all our own.

Here, however, is the surest and easiest solution to this question: these are not common gifts of nature, but special graces of God, which he bestows variously and in a certain measure upon men otherwise wicked. For this reason, we are not afraid, in common parlance, to call this man wellborn, that one depraved in nature. Yet we do not hesitate to include both under the universal condition of human depravity; but we point out what special grace the Lord has bestowed upon the one, while not deigning to bestow it upon the other. When he wished to put Saul over the kingdom he "formed him as a new man" [1 Sam. 10:6]. This is the reason why Plato, alluding to the Homeric legend, says that kings' sons are born with some distinguishing mark. For God, in providing for the human race, often endows with a heroic nature those destined to command.

Private individuals are to be judged in the same way. But because, however excellent anyone has been, his own ambition always pushes him on – a blemish with which all virtues are so sullied that before God they lose all favor – anything in profane men that appears praiseworthy must be considered worthless. Besides, where there is no zeal to glorify God, the chief part of uprightness is absent; a zeal of which all those whom he has not regenerated by his Spirit are devoid. There is good reason for the statement in Isaiah, that "the spirit of the fear of God rests" upon Christ [Isa. 11:2]. By this we are taught that all estranged from Christ lack "the fear of God," which "is the beginning of wisdom" [Ps. 111:10]. As for the virtues that deceive us with their vain show, they shall have their praise in the political assembly and in common renown among men; but before the heavenly judgment seat they shall be of no value to acquire righteousness.

5. Man sins of necessity, but without compulsion

We might add, in our day, great philanthropists like a Bill Gates, Warren Buffet or John D. Rockerfeller; or celebrity examples of compassion e.g. Bob Geldof or Lady Diana. Calvin would regard these examples, as well as such initiatives as 'Children in Need', as gifts of God's common grace, for which we ought to thank Him.

Who has not quietly congratulated themselves – without any thought of gratitude towards God – on a 'job well done'? Who has not, as a result, concluded that they are somehow superior or more worthy of esteem than others?

The basic thought of section 5 is that humankind sins of necessity, but without compulsion (i.e. no one forces us). Calvin argues:

a) People are powerless to move towards good by themselves: Scripture ascribes such movement entirely to God's grace.

b) In their fallen state the will remains eager to sin; "to will is human, to will ill is from our corrupt nature, to will well is of grace."

> *c)* We need to distinguish between necessity and compulsion. To illustrate the distinction, Calvin reflects on God and the devil and then applies the distinction to us:
>
> > *1. God is unable to do evil, not because of compulsion, but because of his boundless goodness: God's free will is not impaired or hindered by the fact that He must do good.*
> >
> > *2. The devil can only do evil, but sins with his will (he necessarily sins, but not because anyone compels him to)*
> >
> > *3. Humankind, though subject to the necessity of sinning, still sins willingly.*
>
> *d)* So, in the Fall humankind sinned willingly and eagerly, not under compulsion from without; their depraved nature can now be moved or impelled only to evil. It is subject to the necessity of sinning.

Because of the bondage of sin by which the will is held bound, it cannot move toward good, much less apply itself thereto; for a movement of this sort is the beginning of conversion to God, which in Scripture is ascribed entirely to God's grace. So Jeremiah prayed to the Lord to be "converted" if it were his will to "convert him" [Jer. 31:18]. Hence the prophet in the same chapter, describing the spiritual redemption of the believing folk, speaks of them as "redeemed from the hand of one stronger than they" [v. 11]. By this he surely means the tight fetters with which the sinner is bound so long as, forsaken by the Lord, he lives under the devil's yoke.

Nonetheless the will remains, with the most eager inclination disposed and hastening to sin. For man, when he gave himself over to this necessity, was not deprived of will, but of soundness of will. Not inappropriately Bernard teaches that to will is in us all: but to will good is gain; to will evil, loss. Therefore simply to will is of man; to will ill, of a corrupt nature; to will well, of grace.

Quoting from Bernard of Clairvaux, *Concerning Grace and Free Will* vi. 6.

Bernard of Clairvaux
(1090 – 20 August 1153)
was a French abbot. For a helpful study on how Calvin draws on Bernard and Augustine on the question of free will, check out Tony Lane's article, *"Did Calvin believe in Free Will?"* which is available online.

Now, when I say that the will bereft of freedom is of necessity either drawn or led into evil, it is a wonder if this seems a hard saying to anyone, since it has nothing incongruous or alien to the usage of holy men. But it offends those who know not how to distinguish between necessity and compulsion. Suppose someone asks them: Is not God of necessity good? Is not the devil of necessity evil? What will they reply? God's goodness is so connected with his divinity that it is no more necessary for him to be God than for him to be good. But the devil by his fall was so cut off from participation in good that he can do nothing but evil.

But suppose some blasphemer sneers that God deserves little praise for His own goodness, constrained as He is to preserve it. Will this not be a ready answer to him: not from violent impulsion, but from His boundless goodness comes God's inability to do evil? Therefore, if the fact that he must do good does not hinder God's free will in doing good; if the devil, who can do only evil, yet sins with his will – who shall say that man therefore sins less willingly because he is subject to the necessity of sinning? Augustine everywhere speaks of this necessity; and even though Caelestius caviled against him invidiously, he did not hesitate to affirm it in these words: "Through freedom man came to be in sin, but the corruption which followed as punishment turned freedom into necessity." And whenever he makes mention of the matter, he does not hesitate to speak in this manner of the necessary bondage of sin.

Quoting from Augustine, On Man's Perfection in Righteousness iv. 9.

The chief point of this distinction, then, must be that man, as he was corrupted by the Fall, sinned willingly, not unwillingly or by compulsion; by the most eager inclination of his heart, not by forced compulsion; by the prompting of his own lust, not by compulsion from without. Yet so depraved is his nature that he can be moved or impelled only to evil. But if this is true, then it is clearly expressed that man is surely subject to the necessity of sinning.

As Francis Schaeffer often said (for example 'The God Who is There', section 3, chapter 4), If we deny personal responsibility for sin, we do two things: a) shift the blame onto someone or something else and b) fall into the 'determinism' camp which effectively robs man of his dignity and worth, making him a 'zero', that is, no more than a bundle of chemicals and brain impulses.

As David comments upon his own sinful nature in Psalm 51, he knows himself to be sinful from birth.

Bernard, agreeing with Augustine, so writes: "Among all living beings man alone is free; and yet because sin has intervened he also undergoes a kind of violence, but of will, not of nature, so that not even thus is he deprived of his innate freedom. For what is voluntary is also free." And a little later: "In some base and strange way the will itself, changed for the worse by sin, makes a necessity for itself. Hence, neither does necessity, although it is of the will, avail to excuse the will, nor does the will, although it is led astray, avail to exclude necessity. For this necessity is as it were voluntary."

Afterward he says that we are oppressed by no other yoke than that of a kind of voluntary servitude. Therefore we are miserable as to servitude and inexcusable as to will because the will, when it was free, made itself the slave of sin. Yet he concludes: "Thus the soul, in some strange and evil way, under a certain voluntary and wrongly free necessity is at the same time enslaved and free: enslaved because of necessity; free because of will. And what is at once stranger and more deplorable, it is guilty because it is free, and enslaved because it is guilty, and as a consequence enslaved because it is free."

Surely my readers will recognize that I am bringing forth nothing new, for it is something that Augustine taught of old with the agreement of all the godly, and it was still retained almost a thousand years later in monastic cloisters. But Lombard, since he did not know how to distinguish necessity from compulsion, gave occasion for a pernicious error.

In this paragraph and the next, Calvin is saying, in a nutshell, that Adam and Eve used their freedom to sin, so incurred true moral guilt before God and additionally became slaves to sin. As people descended from them, our souls (minds and wills) sin because we want to (voluntary) and because we cannot help it (necessity). Our 'freedom' since the fall consists in the freedom to sin as slaves to sin.

Bernard, *Sermons on the Song of Songs* lxxxi. 7, 9.

Peter Lombard (1096-1160) argued that we tend towards evil but have a free will still capable of choosing good. Calvin's response was that our 'free will' still tragically always chooses evil. For that reason he doesn't think "free will" is a very helpful term: "What purpose is served by labelling with a proud name such a slight thing. A noble freedom indeed – for man not to be forced to sin, yet to be such a willing slave that his will is bound by the fetters of sin." (Institutes II.2.7.)

6. Men's inability to do good manifests itself above all in the work of redemption, which God does quite alone

The critical point for our ministry is reached here, for the remedy to people's sin sickness comes from the Great Physician himself. We are entirely dependent on God's working in people's hearts if they would be born again of the Spirit. The only co-operation the Bible allows is us praying for and witnessing to such. The new birth is a work of grace alone.

This work of God is referred to as regeneration, on which, compare and contrast Dr Who:

When he's regenerated, Dr Who is externally transformed, but more or less the same on the inside. On the other hand, Christian regeneration is only an inward (the Already) not an outward transformation (the Not Yet). Outwardly we'll be transformed at the Resurrection.

See for example how God converted Lydia, Acts 16:14. Or the Gentiles at Pisidian Antioch, Acts 13:46.

Compare the miracles of Jesus which illustrate this inability: the man with the withered hand was incapable of restoring his hand. Jesus tells him to stretch it out and through his healing power it is perfectly restored. Likewise our wills and minds and hearts must be completely restored to health.

On the other hand, it behooves us to consider the sort of remedy by which divine grace corrects and cures the corruption of nature. Since the Lord in coming to our aid bestows upon us what we lack, when the nature of his work in us appears, our destitution will, on the other hand, at once be manifest. When the apostle tells the Philippians he is confident "that he who began a good work in you will bring it to completion at the day of Jesus Christ" [Phil. 1:6], there is no doubt that through "the beginning of a good work" he denotes the very origin of conversion itself, which is in the will. God begins his good work in us, therefore, by arousing love and desire and zeal for righteousness in our hearts; or, to speak more correctly, by bending, forming, and directing, our hearts to righteousness.

He completes his work, moreover, by confirming us to perseverance. In order that no one should make an excuse that good is initiated by the Lord to help the will which by itself is weak, the Spirit elsewhere declares what the will, left to itself, is capable of doing: "A new heart shall I give you, and will put a new spirit within you; and I will remove the heart of stone from your flesh, and give you a heart of flesh. And I shall put my spirit within you, and cause you to walk in my statutes" [Ezek. 36:26-27]. Who shall say that the infirmity of the human will is strengthened by his help in order that it may aspire effectively to the choice of good, when it must rather be wholly transformed and renewed?

If in a stone there is such plasticity that, made softer by some means, it becomes somewhat bent, I will not deny that man's heart can be molded to obey the right, provided what is imperfect in him be supplied by God's grace. But if by this comparison the Lord wished to show that nothing good can ever be wrung from our heart, unless it become wholly other, let us not divide between him and us what he claims for himself alone. If, therefore, a stone is transformed into flesh when God converts us to zeal for the right, whatever is of our own will is effaced. What takes its place is wholly from God. I say that the will is effaced; not in so far as it is will, for in man's conversion what belongs to his primal nature remains entire. I also say that it is created anew; not meaning that the will now begins to exist, but that it is changed from an evil to a good will. I affirm that this is wholly God's doing, for according to the testimony of the same apostle, "we are not even capable of thinking" [2 Cor. 3:5]. Therefore he states in another place that God not only assists the weak will or corrects the depraved will, but also works in us to will [Phil. 2:13].

From this, one may easily infer, as I have said, that everything good in the will is the work of grace alone. In this sense he says elsewhere: "It is God who works all things in all" [1 Cor. 12:6]. There he is not discussing universal governance, but is uttering praise to the one God for all good things in which believers excel. Now by saying "all" he surely makes God the author of spiritual life from beginning to end. Previously he had taught the same thing in other words: that believers are from God in Christ [Eph. 1:1; 1 Cor. 8:6].

Here he clearly commends the new creation, which sweeps away everything of our common nature. We ought to understand here an antithesis between Adam and Christ, which he explains more clearly in another place, where he teaches that "we are his workmanship, created in Christ for good works, which God prepared beforehand, that we should walk in them" [Eph. 2:10]. For he would prove our salvation a free gift [cf. Eph. 2:5], because the beginning of every good is from the second creation, which we attain in Christ.

And yet if even the least ability came from ourselves, we would also have some share of the merit. But Paul, to strip us, argues that we deserve nothing because "we have been created in Christ ... for good works which God prepared beforehand" [Eph. 2:10]. He means by these words that all parts of good works from their first impulse belong to God. In this way the prophet, after saying in the psalm that we are God's handiwork, so that we may not share it with him, immediately adds: "And we ourselves have not done it" [Ps. 100:3]. It is clear from the context that he is speaking of regeneration, which is the beginning of the spiritual life; for he goes on to say that "we are his people, and the sheep of his pasture" [Ps. 100:3]. Moreover, we see how, not simply content to have given God due praise for our salvation, he expressly excludes us from all participation in it. It is as if he were saying that not a whit remains to man to glory in, for the whole of salvation comes from God. ▶

The first French edition of 1541 adds: 'From the first moment of our conversion to our final perseverance, all the good we do is from God in every part.' Calvin then adds further testimony from Ps 100.3 where the Psalmist praises God because his people are chosen by him to be the sheep of his pasture, implying that he not only chose them, but that he leads them to their final destination (heaven) and into his very presence thanks to his mercy and truth, ("love and faithfulness"). All the credit goes to God because He is the one who saves us from beginning to end.

HOW CAN IT BE WRONG IF I CAN'T HELP IT?

Kirsten Birkett explores

addiction and sin through

the lens of Augustine

Saint Augustine (1650) by Philippe de Champaigne

WHY WRITE ABOUT ADDICTION AND SIN?

"Addiction is a brain disease."
David J. Nutt and Liam J. Nestor, *Addiction* (Oxford: Oxford University Press, 2013), 1.

In a book recently published by Oxford University Press as a summary of current research and thinking about addiction, the very first line on page one puts addiction in its place. It is a brain disease: an illness, a sickness, something wrong with you physiologically. This is what we know after years of scientific research. How can we put such an archaic, and judgmental, term as 'sin' next to this?

There are certainly voices that would object strongly to the very idea of putting addiction and sin together. If addiction is an illness, a matter of physiological brain changes which make the addict unable to think straight or process desires properly – and there is certainly strong evidence that such is the case – then the addict is no more sinful than the person with measles. It is a disease, not a sin. Yet even within the scientific literature, the picture is not always so clear. Substance addiction certainly affects self-control and low levels of self-control may be a predictor of addictive behaviour; but self-control can be regained, albeit with help, once the addict chooses to engage in therapy. What is the role of choice, then, in addiction? If I cannot help but have another drink because my cravings are simply overwhelming, am I culpable for my drunkenness? If my addiction means I can think of nothing but how to get my next hit of a drug, am I really responsible for the loss of self-control that ensues when I take it? Or for anything I do under its influence?

Nutt and Nestor, *vii*.

American Psychiatric Association, *Diagnostic and Statistical Manual of Mental Disorders*, 5th edition (Washington DC and London: American Psychiatric Publishing, 2013), 481.

This is an important area, for the sake of those who are addicts and desperately need help, as well as for our own right thinking about God, our created nature, and sin. We need to get our categories straight. It is important to talk about what addiction is, and what sin is, and precisely where we think they overlap.

To understand addiction I have looked to current research as well as medical definitions. Science is always evolving, and brain science is still in its early stages; nonetheless, recent discoveries have uncovered a lot of new information about how addiction manifests at the physical level. To understand sin, we will be looking at Augustine of Hippo's treatment of it; not just because he is faithful to the Bible as he discusses sin, but the way in which he construes sin is, I think, particularly helpful when we think about addiction.

It is not just the question of whether having an addiction is in itself sinful. More than that, a better understanding of sin and an awareness of the parallels with addiction will give us important categories and distinctions that can help us understand how to think of addiction and to help those suffering from such a condition. Thinking about addiction in these categories also has a further important benefit. We are all sinners. Any sin is one for which we are both culpable and yet, without God's grace, we cannot help but do. Thinking about addiction, then, takes us beyond the problems of addiction and addicts, to all of us. We are all by nature addicted to our selfish desires, whether or not that manifests in particular substance abuse. Those of us who do not run into diagnosable addiction may be less obvious in our sin; but it is still there. Non-addicts can never be judgmental towards addicts. Understanding addiction, therefore, helps us understand ourselves.

WHAT IS ADDICTION?

DSM-5 has been criticised as being overly influenced by drug companies, and by over-medicalising disorders which may have other aspects of causation. Nevertheless, as far as I am aware there are no particular objections to the bulk of what DSM-5 says about substance abuse.

Our first port of call is the *Diagnostic and Statistical Manual of Mental Disorders*, 5th edition (*DSM-5*), the official publication of the American Psychiatric Association, as its standard for diagnosing mental problems. What does this authoritative work have to say about addiction?

DSM-5, 485.

Actually, nothing. *DSM-5* (as with previous editions) specifically does not label any condition an 'addiction.' This is deliberate: the word 'addiction' is not used as a diagnostic term "because of its uncertain definition and its potentially negative connotation." What are we to make of this? At the very least, a common understanding of addiction as being a definite syndrome, and one beyond one's control, would seem to be too simplistic.

Although the section heading is 'Substance-related and addictive disorders', DSM-5, 481-589. The authors do not specify what the potentially negative connotation is.

Instead, *DSM-5* includes 'substance-use disorders' – conditions where the use of the drug is itself considered pathological – and 'substance-induced disorders' – harmful conditions that may result from use of a drug (intoxication, withdrawal and other induced mental disorders such as psychosis or depression). In other words,

Ten classes of drugs are listed: alcohol, caffeine, cannabis, hallucinogens, inhalants, opioids, sedatives, hypnotics and anxiolytics, stimulants (amphetamine-type substances, cocaine and other stimulants), tobacco, and 'other or unknown substances.' Not all drugs are equal in this list; so, for instance, there is no such thing as a caffeine 'substance use disorder', only 'substance-induced disorders': caffeine intoxication (involving extremely high doses) and withdrawal from caffeine intoxication can be harmful.

DSM-5 remains deliberately agnostic as to whether a person can be *addicted* (Latin: *addictio*, enslaved) to or by a substance. The question of culpability is avoided. For most researchers in the field, however, the common term 'addiction' is used, even when judgments about culpability, or even cause, are withheld. That said, what are we to understand addiction actually *is*?

ADDICTION / SUBSTANCE ABUSE IS AN ILLNESS OF THE BRAIN

DSM-5 describes substance-use disorder as fundamentally a misuse or co-option of the reward mechanisms of the brain; the parts of the brain that encourage us to do certain activities (such as eating) which are good for us. What the drugs do is take over those systems, encouraging people that what they really want is the drug. Substances of addiction are highly rewarding, because they trigger far higher levels of dopamine – which affects how good we feel – than those triggered by food or water or other natural rewards.

DSM-5, 481.

Kenneth Blum, Mary Hauser, James Fratantonio, Rajendra D. Badgaiyan, 'Molecular Genetic Testing in Pain and Addiction: Facts, Fiction and Clinical Utility,' *Addiction Genetics*, 1 (2015):19-23, 20; Nutt and Lestor, 22.

We are also creatures who seek goals, and our goal-seeking circuitry can similarly be hijacked by substance-related *cues* (places or people associated with drug-taking, for instance). Addicts show hyperactivity in the part of the brain involved in goal-directed behaviour during cue-induced craving, and during withdrawal. The effect of long-term use of the drug can also override those parts of the brain necessary for optimal decision-making.

Nutt and Lestor, 23.

At the same time, any linking between motivation and rewards must be learned and encoded in memory, and there is evidence that dopamine is involved in learning and memory. Dopamine is also involved in making predictions about future rewards. Because addictive drugs increase dopamine, the drug will therefore make it easier to remember drug use and how rewarding it is.

Nutt and Lestor, 24.

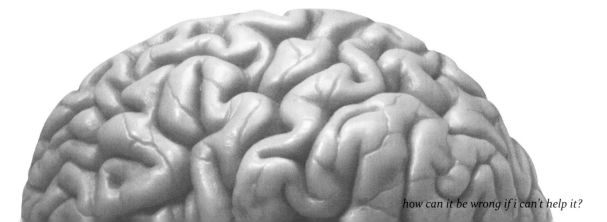

ADDICTION IS A BEHAVIOUR

Nonetheless, while brain malfunction is increasingly the accepted pattern of what underlies addiction, the diagnostic categories are still primarily behavioural. What constitutes an addiction is not just a state of the brain, but the choices people make. So even in DSM-5, criticised for 'over-medicalising' mental issues, choice and behaviour are clear factors in understanding substance abuse: "Overall, the diagnosis of a substance use disorder is based on a pathological pattern of behaviours related to use of the substance." These behaviours include such things as trying to cut down but failing, experiencing cravings, social impairment (with continued use despite the problems the substance causes), and increased tolerance and withdrawal.

DSM-5, 483.

What we call 'addiction', then, basically involves deliberate, high-volume use of a dangerous substance despite being fully aware of its negative effects. It is not just the taking of the drug that constitutes the abuse, nor just the negative effects; it is the behaviour of continuing to use the drug, even in the knowledge of how bad it is.

ADDICTION IS (AT LEAST PARTLY) GENETICALLY DETERMINED

It is notable that the DSM definition is almost entirely behavioural. Nonetheless, DSM-5 also recognises that there is a genetic predisposition to substance-use disorders; even when children of alcoholics are adopted at birth, they are still three to four times as likely as others to become alcoholic themselves. Other family studies have similar conclusions.

DSM-5, 494.

Rohan H. C. Palmer, Leslie Brick, Nicole R. Nugent, L. Cinnamon Bidwell, John E. McGeary, Valerie S. Knopik and Matthew C. Keller, 'Examining the Role of Common Genetic Variants on Alcohol, Tobacco, Cannabis and Illicit Drug Dependence: Genetics of Vulnerability to Drug Dependence', *Addiction*, 110 (2014): 530-537. Nutt and Nestor claim that twin registry and adoption studies suggest that the heritability of alcoholism may be as high as 50-60%, p85. Of course, this also means that 40-50% of people with the same DNA do not develop alcoholism.

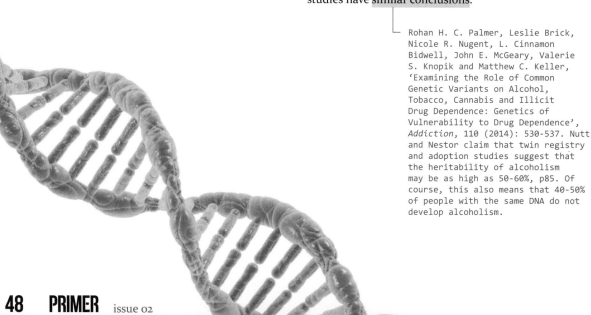

Indeed, there is a lot of evidence that suggests there is a genetic component in addictions, or behaviour that seems likely to lead to addiction. Various studies certainly seem to support the idea that the body and brain you are born with at least predisposes you to something like addiction, even if not causing it.

Blum *et al*; Michael Slezak, 'Having Trouble Giving up Smoking? Blame your Genes', *New Scientist*, Issue 3050, 5 December 2015.

CAN YOU BE ADDICTED TO SOMETHING BEHAVIOURAL?

So far the discussion has concerned drugs to which people become addicted. However, it is common to speak of behavioural addictions: being addicted to the gym, or shopping, or whatever. Are behavioural addictions real?

The NHS certainly thinks so, listing spending addiction, gambling addiction, and food addiction (over- or under-eating); even sex and love addictions. This is based on the fact that the behavioural symptoms can be similar to drug addiction, as well as some evidence that the neural changes are similar. Other sources speak of a similar list of behavioural addictions. *DSM-5* has controversially included gambling for the first time, but specifically relegates other behavioural 'addictions' (internet gaming, sex, shopping and exercise) to a less certain status, since the research is less clear.

www.beatingaddictions.co.uk/am-i-dependent-have-i-got-addiction.html

www.nhs.uk/Livewell/addiction/Pages/sexandloveaddiction.aspx

Nutt and Nestor, 85.

One of the complaints made against *DSM-5* was regarding the inclusion of 'behavioural' addictions (gambling) where previously only substance abuse was included in this section.

DSM-5, 481.

ADDICTION DEVELOPS

While the disease model dominates in discussion of addiction, another facet of understanding addiction is seeing the ways in which it is *not* like other physical diseases caused by (say) bacteria or viruses. Addiction is not 'caught'; it develops. It is possible to use addictive drugs, even regularly, without being addicted. Drinking, even daily, even with occasional intoxication, is not enough for a diagnosis of alcoholism.

DSM-5, 496.

Addiction has several recognisable stages. The initial motive might be seeking a thrill, or escaping pain. The drug gives temporary satiation of the desire; indeed, can feel wonderful. Following the initial effects, a preoccupation with the substance may emerge, with excessive thoughts about it, and excessive time spent planning to use it. Time thinking about the drug spills over into other aspects of life. Less time is spent on other activities.

Tolerance and withdrawal contribute to this. As tolerance develops, more of the substance is needed to achieve the same effect. Withdrawal can be extremely painful, and so motivation to take the drug again increases; now the drug is not just fulfilling the original need, it has the added effect of taking away withdrawal symptoms. Cravings develop, but sometimes tolerance gets to the point that satisfying them becomes impossible.

Whatever the reason for the initial decision to take the drug, even if it was undertaken freely and deliberately – and even if ongoing, conscious choices to continue taking the drug are free and deliberate – the drugs clearly cause physiological changes in the brain that mean the urge to continue can seem overwhelming. Once the brain reward circuitry is compromised, the compulsion for the drug can occur even without conscious feelings of pleasure. Addicts can genuinely feel out of control, compelled to take the drug.

Some people say the substance gives them meaning; they only feel 'real' when under the influence. It makes them feel normal. This is particularly common in opiate and alcohol addiction, and can make abstinence particularly hard because the person never feels fully complete without the drug.

Nutt and Nestor, 17.

To conclude, addiction is not a simple concept. It seems that it involves both chosen behaviours, and physiological compulsion. It may begin in a genetic predisposition, as well as intense psychological motivation. A person may feel that there is genuinely no choice in his or her drug use. A drug user can feel blamed by judgmental people who call it sin; or may be encouraged by an 'over-medicalised' disease model to deny responsibility for what is irresponsible behaviour. All of these are true, and naïve reductionism is to be avoided on any side.

Historians of the science of addiction, for instance, often reject the medical and scientific model of addiction as being crudely reductive, ignoring culturally specific phenomena, and invoking 'biological essentialism and naïve positivism.' David T. Courtwright, 'Addiction and the Science of History', *Addiction*, 107 (2012): 486-492, p489.

However, while the science may be accurate, a scientific description alone is never complete. We now need to turn our attention to exactly what we mean by 'sin.'

UNDERSTANDING SIN: AUGUSTINE AND 'THE CITY OF GOD'

Augustine of Hippo published *Concerning the City of God against the Pagans* around 426 AD, as his mature reflection on how Christianity differs from pagan philosophy, and giving an exposition of history from a biblical viewpoint. As such, it also functions as a kind of systematic theology, although topics are not discussed under subject headings, but as they appear in his chronology. The story of history, as Augustine sees it, is the story of two branches of humanity (which he describes as two cities): those who live by human standards, and those who live according to God's will. Those who live by human standards, by definition, are living in sin, and are utterly culpable for it:

All quotations here are taken from the Penguin Books edition (London, 2003), translated by Henry Bettenson; page numbers refer to that edition.

Now the reign of death has held mankind in such utter subjection that they would all be driven headlong into that second death, which has no ending, as their well-deserved punishment, if some were not rescued from it by the underserved grace of God.

Augustine, XIV.1, 547.

Bondage to sin and death is the way that humankind lives after the fall. What, then, is sin?

Pride, Augustine says, is the first manifestation of a sinful will, the start of every kind of sin. It means taking oneself as the fundamental measure and purpose of human existence. It abandons God as the basis on which the mind should be fixed, to become based on oneself; it over-values oneself. It is a voluntary desertion of God.

This pride both consists of and creates disordered love. It begins in the wrong kind of self-love; not loving oneself as God does, as a creature, but loving oneself above all else. This idea of what one loves is fundamental to Augustine's understanding of sin, and the difference between the two cities.

Augustine,
XV.13, 593.

We see then that the two cities were created by two kinds of love: the earthly city was created by self-love reaching the point of contempt for God, the Heavenly City by the love of God carried as far as contempt of self. In fact, the earthly city glories in itself, the Heavenly City glories in the Lord. The former looks for glory from men, the latter finds its highest glory in God, the witness of a good conscience. The earthly lifts up its head in its own glory, the Heavenly City says to its God: 'My glory; you lift up my head.' In the former, the lust for domination lords it over its princes as over the nations it subjugates; in the other both those put in authority and those subject to them serve one another in love, the rulers by their counsel, the subjects by obedience. The one city loves its own strength shown in its powerful leaders; the other says to its God, 'I will love you, my Lord, my strength.'

See Matt Jenson, *The Gravity of Sin: Augustine, Luther and Barth* on 'homo incurvatus in se' (T&T Clark, London, 2006), 7.

Sin is disordered love, because it loves the wrong things and is also disordered *will*; the will is turned to what is evil, and lesser, rather than to what is good, and greater. This creates fundamental disorder, because we were created to live for, and to love God; but pride instead turns to the self, and so we choose what is created instead of the creator. While these things might be good, we are choosing them in an evil way, because we value them more than we value God.

Augustine,
XII.8, 480.

I likewise know that when an evil choice happens in any being, then what happens is dependent on the will of that being; the failure is voluntary, not necessary, and the punishment that follows is just. For this failure does not consist in defection to things which are evil in themselves; it is the defection in itself that is evil. That is, it is not a falling away to evil natures; the defection is evil in itself, as a defection from him who supremely exists to something of a lower degree of reality; and this is contrary to the order of nature.

2. SIN IS FALSEHOOD

Because sin lives for the wrong thing, it lives a lie. If we lived by the standard of truth we live by God's standard; but when we live by our own standards, we live by falsehood. This is a necessary consequence of rejecting our created order. We were originally created good, and righteous, and were meant to live by the standards of our creator; not carrying out our own will, but our creator's. Falsehood consists in not living in the way for which we were created.

Augustine, XIV.4, 552.

Consequently, every particular sin involves a falsehood.

Augustine, XIV.4, 553.

For sin only happens by an act of will; and our will is for our own welfare, or for the avoidance of misfortune. And hence the falsehood: we commit sin to promote our welfare, and it results instead in our misfortune; or we sin to increase our welfare, and the result is rather to increase our misfortune. What is the reason for this, except that well-being can only come to man from God, not from himself? And he forsakes God by sinning, and he sins by living by his own standard.

This self-rule, which is now the rule of humanity, means we actually live like the Devil.

Augustine, XIV.4, 552.

Thus, when man lives 'by the standard of man' and not 'by the standard of God', he is like the Devil; because even an angel should not have lived by the angel's standard, but by God's so as to stand firm in the truth and speak the truth that comes from God's truth, not the lie that derives from his own falsehood.

Living by the rule of self is living a lie.

3. SIN IS BAD FOR US

We were not created for sin. It violates our creation, and so sin will necessarily have bad effects on us. When we live in a way contrary to God's way, we will suffer, as we are going against our own design. In fact, when we become less than what we were created to be, Augustine says, we become less real; we actually move towards uncreation. It is *inclinatus ad se*, turning towards oneself.

Augustine, XIV.13, 572.

Yet man did not fall away to the extent of losing all being; but when he had turned towards himself his being was less real than when he adhered to him who exists in a supreme degree. And so, to abandon God and to exist in oneself, that is to please oneself, is not immediately to lose all being; but it is to come nearer to nothingness.

This is a cruel irony. In sin, humanity tried to exalt itself above God instead of remaining humble before him. However the result was the exact opposite. If we had remained content to be humble, we would have been properly exalted, even like gods. In grasping greatness, however, we became debased, going against our created nature. Devout humility, Augustine says, actually makes the mind subject to what is superior. Self-exaltation, in contrast, spurns subjection and falls away from God, which means being lower.

Augustine, XIV.13, 573.

We can see then that the Devil would not have entrapped man by the obvious and open sin of doing what God had forbidden, had not man already started to please himself. That is why he was delighted also with the statement, 'You will be like gods' (Gen 3:5). In fact they would have been better able to be like gods if they had in obedience adhered to the supreme and real ground of their being, if they had not in pride made themselves their own ground. For created gods are gods not in their own true nature but by participation in the true God. By aiming at more, a man is diminished, when he elects to be self-sufficient and defects from the one who is really sufficient for him.

In sinning, we hurt ourselves. We become less, far less than what we might have been. We become less than ourselves. Being disordered leads to further disorder, as one becomes less real.

4. HAVING FALLEN, WE CAN'T HELP BUT SIN, AND SO DO WHAT IS BAD FOR US

Augustine, XIV.11, 568.

And the consequent deeds were evil because they followed the will's own line, and not God's.

Part of the consequence of Adam and Eve's original sin was that humanity was cast into a fallen world with their now disordered natures. Sin means we have fallen into slavery. God has handed us over to ourselves, but it is not the freedom we were grasping for. On the contrary, freedom was in the garden, living out our created natures freely. Now, we find ourselves in slavery.

Augustine, XIV.15, 574-5.

Among other things, such as the judgment that sin deserves, Augustine brings out the subjective cost of such a life. In blunt terms, living this way means that we are unhappy. Slavery, falsehood and unhappiness go together:

Augustine,
XIV.4, 552-3.

Man has undoubtedly the will to be happy, even when he pursues happiness by living in a way which makes it impossible of attainment. What could be more of a falsehood than a will like that? Hence we can say with meaning that every sin is a falsehood. For sin only happens by an act of will; and our will is for our own welfare, or for the avoidance of misfortune. And hence the falsehood: we commit sin to promote our welfare, and it results instead in our misfortune; or we sin to increase our welfare, and the result is rather to increase our misfortune.

One might say this is a perfect description of addiction.

5. THE BODY DOES NOT MAKE US SIN, FALSE SELF-LOVE DOES

Augustine wrote in a context in which a number of competing philosophies agreed that the body is fundamentally evil or tainted, and the source of evil. Christianity, however, is positive about creation and embodiedness. The body, Augustine says, cannot *cause* sin. The body is good.

However in Augustine's time, as in ours, some of the biblical language can be confusing in this regard; in particular, the biblical refrain of "living according to the flesh", is clearly a negative thing. Augustine asserts that this does not mean denying that bodily creation is good. In Galatians 5:19-21, the works of the flesh are not just sensual pleasures, although some are (fornication, impurity, drunkenness); but they also include faults of the mind (devotion to idols, sorcery, enmity, quarrelsomeness, jealously, animosity, etc.). In fact devotion to an idol might mean you refrain from sensual pleasure, but that is still living by the rule of the flesh.

Augustine, XIV.1, 547.

Sin, then, is not associated with flesh meaning 'physical body.' Rather, sin arises in the soul. It is not the case that the flesh is the cause of every kind of moral failing. This shows a failure to consider man's nature carefully. We are weighed down by the corruptible body, true, but the cause of our being weighed down is not the "true nature and substance" of our body but its corruption.

Augustine, XIV.3, 550.

Augustine, XIV.3, 551.

This means that Augustine can both acknowledge the weakness of the body, and its role in temptation, while denying that the body is ever the *cause* of sin. Rather, sin is the cause of the bodily weakness which, post-fall, we now all inherit.

No doubt this corruption of the flesh results in some incitements to wrongdoing and in actual vicious longings; yet we must not attribute to the flesh all the faults of a wicked life, which would mean that we absolve the Devil of all those faults, since he has no flesh... It is in fact not by the possession of flesh, which the Devil does not possess, that man has become like the Devil; it is by living by the rule of self, that is by the rule of man.

Augustine,
XIV.3, 551-2.

6. WITH GRACE WE CAN REPENT

The great message that those in the City of God have discovered – the same message that would inspire Luther centuries later – is the rescue that God provides through his grace, in the death of Christ. Even the slavery of sin, which willpower cannot break, is not the final sentence.

So all men are dead in sin, without any exception at all... And for all these dead, there died the one man truly alive... so that we may put our faith in him who justifies the irreligious.

Augustine,
XX.6, 904.

In short, in Augustine we find a description of sin that reminds us that the real addiction, the real slavery to our desires, is sin itself. Sin is our longing for something that we seek in the wrong place. Like addiction, sin is our seeking freedom, but getting slavery. It is our seeking exaltation and bliss, but getting pain and dissatisfaction. This is what the original sin was; and it is what we continue to do, of necessity - until, of course, by grace we are enabled to change. Even the grip of sin itself can be conquered by grace. In that lies the hope for all addicts.

LIKE ADDICTION, SIN IS
OUR SEEKING FREEDOM,
BUT GETTING SLAVERY.
IT IS OUR SEEKING
EXALTATION AND BLISS,
BUT GETTING PAIN
AND DISSATISFACTION.

The CCEF website provides excellent material in this regard: *www.ccef.org*

This is not an article about treatment for addiction. There is plenty of good literature available, from Christian and non-Christian sources. However, given our discussion it is worth drawing out a few implications for pastoral practice.

Addiction is not necessarily sin, but probably involves sin

Addiction, insofar as it is purely a state of impaired brain chemistry, is not itself sin. Babies can be born addicted to heroin because of the heroin use of the mother. Nonetheless, most addicts are not born that way. Addiction is something that develops with habitual use of the substance (or activity) of abuse; a person chose to take an illegal drug, or drink to drunkenness repeatedly – that is, to do something in itself sinful. Addiction is manifested in ongoing choices to serve the desire rather than serve God.

Recovery will be difficult and will take time

Carlo C. DiClemente, Addiction and Change: How Addictions Develop and Addicted People Recover, (New York and London: The Guildford Press, 2003), vii.

How a society views individuals who engage in addictive behaviours has an important influence on addiction and recovery from addiction. If addiction is seen as a moral failing, it will be condemned. If seen as a deficit in knowledge, it will be educated. If the addiction is viewed as an acceptable aberration, it will be tolerated.

The above quotation, taken from a secular book on treating addictions, reveals what most people expect from any view that sees addiction as a 'moral failing': the treatment is condemnation (and perhaps, nothing more). If this is how the church is perceived to address moral failings in its members, then that is a sad state of affairs indeed.

As we have seen above, there are ways in which we *do* see addiction as a moral failing; even when the physiological aspects of addiction may be viewed as illness, these rarely appear without other aspects which come under the category of sin. Moreover, although there seem to be inherited genetic aspects to addiction that make some people more vulnerable to it than others, addiction rarely happens without sinful activity to trigger it, and it normally results in further sinful behaviour as the cravings it produces are very hard to resist. Yet being 'sin' does not mean that it can be fixed by telling people to try hard to repent. Quite the contrary.

I am assuming in this discussion that the addict will be encouraged to seek any appropriate medical help. The following comments are for pastors who are exercising care above and beyond professional medical advice.

In a fallen world, bodies are weak, and sin has damaging consequences. The further an addiction has progressed, the more difficult it will be to overcome. Some sins are harder to repent of than others, particular when there are bodily changes involved. Education alone is not the answer; as we have seen, it is part of the very definition of addiction that addicts might be entirely aware of the harmfulness of their habits, but still do not stop. This is the case even when a person realises that what he or she is doing is sinful. Simply telling the person to repent, however forcefully and persuasively, is not enough.

Indeed, as most people in pastoral ministry would recognise, this does not make helping someone with an addiction qualitatively different from helping any other sinner. Telling any person 'just trust God', in *any* circumstance, is not enough to help them *do* it. Controlling anger, or forgiving someone who has sinned against you, or refraining from telling lies or gossiping or any other sin, is very hard to do; it takes time and patience and constant repentance. Willpower alone does not get it done. Addiction may be one of the hardest sins to repent of, precisely because of the bodily changes involved, but the process is essentially the same.

We need to understand the heart

Whether we call it identifying underlying patterns of thought, or understanding motivation, or understanding heart issues, knowing what drives an addiction is crucial; and the further 'down' we can trace the causal layers, the better. Understanding why the person became addicted is central to understanding how to help him or her recover. Whether this includes a genetic predisposition or not is beside the point; the fact is, that predisposition came to fruition in a certain way for that person, and that is what drives the behaviour. As Christians, we know that behaviour comes from within, and the complex mix of beliefs, feelings and convictions that constitute 'the heart' lie behind what we do.

There was a time when forceful confrontation was used as part of secular therapy for addiction. It is no longer recommended, not just because the philosophical understanding of addiction has changed, but because it was simply shown not to work. William M. White and William R. Miller, 'The Use of Confrontation in Addiction Treatment: History, Science and Time for a Change', *Counselor*, 8:4 (2007), 12-30.

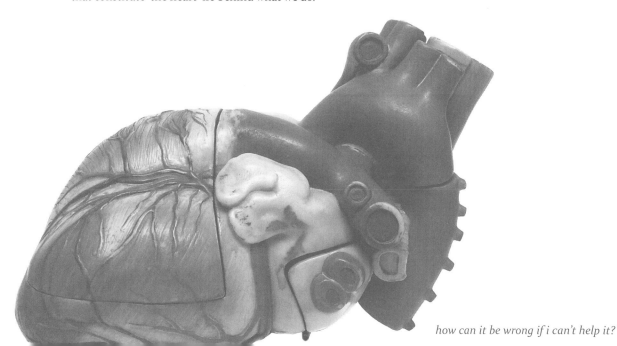

For the counsellor, *listening* is crucial. The addict, like any sinner, will need to be able to express and explore what is in the heart. If heart 'idols' are to be uncovered, the addict needs patient help to talk about and identify what he or she is longing for, and why.

Our approach from the outset ought to be loving and empathetic. The person needs to see the sin for themselves, through questioning, listening, reflecting and guiding to insight. This is a gentle process so that the person, motivated to change, confident that God's Spirit will change them, will see where prayer and repentance needs to be focused. This is enlightening and inspirational when it really happens. It does not happen through hectoring or condemnation. Our capacity for self-deception and defensiveness is too great.

Have a robust doctrine of embodiment

All of our behaviour, internal or external, is bodily in some way. We are embodied beings. Every emotion, every attitude, every thought uses the body and is affected by body chemistry. Our bodies, however, are not in control and need not be.

To say we are tackling emotional/psychological/moral issues is not a denial of underlying neurochemical issues. Every behaviour, thought or impulse has a corresponding neurological substrata. Sometimes it is significantly malfunctioning, and treating it with a drug will help with fixing bad emotions or behaviours. But it works the other way too; changing the thoughts, emotions and actions can change the brain chemistry. The medical solution will never be the only one and, given how incomplete understanding is at the moment, does not come near a full solution.

Can we reconcile models of brain chemistry with the reality that sin comes from the soul? We may never have the complete answer this side of glory, but the fact that brain changes can be identified in addiction need not conflict with our conviction that the root cause is what we might call idolatry. After all, idolaters crave the thing they worship, and give up everything for it. That is precisely how you diagnose idolatry. It is desiring a created thing more than God. A neurochemical explanation does not replace the 'worship' explanation; it simply explains how that particular kind of worship is instantiated in one particular person.

Learn from successful secular models of counselling

There is evidence that the most common secular treatments – CBT, 12-step programmes and other motivational therapies – have virtually identical outcomes across three years. Similarly, drugs such as disulfiram and naltrexone, and others used to treat alcohol and opioid dependence, have similar success rates, which are all quite good. However it is enlightening to see what it is about secular models that seems to work *best*. What makes the difference – what makes any one of these therapies increase its success rate – are "unspecified components such as therapeutic relationship." It seems that the patient's relationship with the counsellor, in some unspecified way, is still the most important aspect of whether therapy will be successful. What is it that marks out a successful counselling relationship? Some things that have been shown to make a difference are expectancy (the counsellor believing that the therapy will work), allegiance (therapists trusting the system they are using), empathy and probably fidelity; whether the client is optimistic about outcomes and is motivated to succeed; and whether the client has a social support network.

This is good news for Christians, and it is good precisely *because* we can see addiction as sin, and not just as illness. Addicts are *not* dependent solely on medical help, which, while having good success rates, is never perfect. The things that have been identified as making all the difference, however – relationships, social support, and belief that change is possible – are precisely those things that Christian communities based around the word of God have.

Cognitive Behavioural Therapy

William R. Miller and Theresa B. Moyers, 'The Forest and the Trees: Relational and Specific Factors in Addiction Treatment', *Addiction* (Monograph Northampton: Society for the Study of Addiction, 2014), 3.

John C. Norcross and Bruce E. Wampold, 'Evidence-based Therapy Relationships: Research Conclusions and Clinical Practices', *Psychotherapy* 48:1 (2011), 98-102, 98.

Miller and Moyers, 6.

ibid., 7.

CONCLUSION

Having a weak body or brain, even one affected by drugs, does not in itself constitute a sin. Giving in to the temptation to serve a physical desire, rather than serve God, *is* sin. However God's grace can help any sinner. We have resources that secular counsellors would love to have. Let us prayerfully, compassionately, and confidently, use them to help addicts, as the sinners that we all are. ⫿

If the whole human race lay in one grave, the epitaph on its headstone might well be: *"It seemed like a good idea at the time."*

Rebecca West, *The New York Times*, October 2, 1977

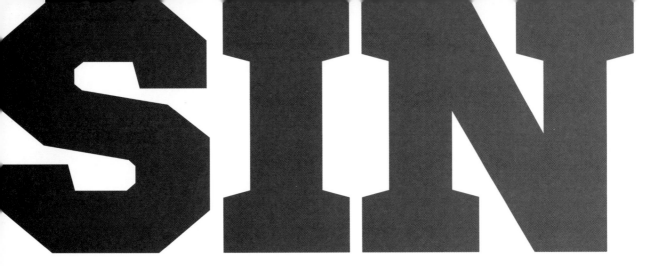

SIN

*The subject of sin raises lots of questions. We can't answer them all in the space of one issue of **Primer**, but we thought we could fire some FAQ's at theologian John Frame and get some short sharp answers.*

What's the difference between temptation and sin?

Sin is disobedience to God's law and therefore violation of our relationship to him. Temptation occurs when someone or something entices us to sin. Temptation can come from Satan (Gen 3) or from our own lusts (Jas 1:14). It is possible to be tempted without committing sin, as Scripture says concerning Jesus (Heb 4:15).

Is desire sinful?

Not in itself. Some desires are good, because they are desires for good things (Ps 10:17, 21:2, 73:25, Prov 11:23, Rom 10:1, 1 Tim 3:1, 1 Pet 2:2). Of course, even good things can become idols, when we desire them more than God. We should desire nothing more than we desire God (Ps 73:25).

John M. Frame, *The Doctrine of the Christian Life* (Phillipsburg, N.J: P & R Publishing, 2012), 846.

As Frame says elsewhere, *"The Bible does not condemn all human desires... Scripture motivates our obedience by promising rewards, thus legitimising our desire of God's blessings. God himself is the chief desire of the believer's heart."* But as Frame says in his discussion of the ten commandments, Jesus does condemn desires which want what God has forbidden (lust for another's spouse, hatred of another being equivalent to murder). So some desires are sinful even if we don't act upon them. In the words of the *Heidelberg Catechism*:

Q 113: What does the tenth Commandment require?
A: That not even the least inclination or thought against any commandment of God ever enter our heart, but that with our whole heart we continually hate all sin and take pleasure in all righteousness.

Q&A

Was Paul *"the worst of sinners"*? Can we all say that?

Paul says he was the least of the apostles because he persecuted the church (1 Cor 15:9). I presume that was the main reason why he described himself as the "worst of sinners" in 1 Tim 1:15 (he does mention some other things there, but those are qualities of all sinners). Does that imply that persecuting the church is the worst possible sin? To say that is to translate Paul's very personal statement into a general ethical principle, in which we compare various sins and combinations of sins in an abstract way. I think to take it that way broadens the context too much. Paul is not interested in comparing all the sins that people might conceivably commit. Rather, he is overwhelmed with his own guilt and God's incredible grace – that God should have chosen, as an *Apostle*, someone who had done the things that Paul had done. He expresses that feeling by saying that he cannot imagine any worse sinner being saved by God's grace. He is the "worst," or the "chief." That is, compared to what he has done, the sins of others can be overlooked.

I think he is also trying to forestall criticism. Someone might claim that he is elevating his own righteousness above that of other people. He wants to put that criticism to rest in advance: In myself, I am no better than anybody else; in fact, I am worse than anyone else I can think of.

Can we say this? Well, we may well find ourselves in the same mood as Paul, contemplating our sins and recognising that when all is said and done we are no better than child rapists or Islamic terrorists. It is then not wrong to speak as Paul does. But it would be wrong 1) to be so preoccupied with this that we should be driven to despair, or 2) to try to incorporate this conclusion into an abstract mathematical system where we try to rank sins at different levels.

SIN

Is there a hierarchy of sins? Are some sins worse than others?

Yes. Some matters in the law are "weightier" (Matt 23:23; cf. Matt 5:19, John 19:11), particularly justice, mercy, and faithfulness. But that fact doesn't excuse us from sin in less weighty matters (same text). So any sin is sufficient to condemn us to hell apart from God's grace (Deut 27:26, Ezek 18:4, 33:8, Rom 5:16). Scripture does distinguish between "unintentional" sins (Lev 4:2-3) and sins committed with a "high hand" (Num 15:22-31) (i.e. where the sinner intentionally defies God's authority), assigning different penalties for these in the law. Steadfast love and the knowledge of God are more important than making sacrifice (Hos 6:6). The worst sin is the blasphemy against the Holy Spirit (Matt 12:31) which Jesus says cannot be forgiven. Wayne Grudem defines this as "malicious, willful rejection and slander against the Holy Spirit's work attesting to Christ, and attributing that work to Satan" (Grudem, *Systematic Theology*, 508).

How does God feel about us when we sin?

God's feelings are very complex. He hates our sin, but continues to love the elect with the eternal love with which he loved them in Christ (Eph 1:3-10). Scripture also says that he hates the wicked (Ps 11:5). That pertains to the non-elect, but also to the elect, before they come to trust in Christ (Eph 2:1-3).

It is also helpful to distinguish God's attitudes toward us according to the two levels I mentioned above. On the first level, he embraces us as the one who has saved us from all our sins. On the second level, he administrates discipline as our loving Father.

Q&A

Why do Christians pray *"forgive us our sins"*? Aren't we forgiven already?

We pray this because the Lord commanded us to (Luke 11:4). Some principles behind this:

1. Our relationship with God has two levels. On the first level, he has forgiven all our sins for Jesus' sake, past, present, and future. That admits us to the family of God. But there is also a second level, because God our Father sets standards for behaviour in the family. Heb 12:7-11 speaks of divine discipline for sin. This occurs, and is actually proof that we are part of his family: else "you are illegitimate children and not sons" (verse 8). That second-level family discipline requires us to order our behaviour. That involves repentance and forgiveness by our Father.

2. Jesus said that that his disciples were clean (first level), but that they still needed to wash their feet (John 13:9, 10). That indicates the relationship between the two levels.

3. If we are truly sons and daughters of God in Jesus, then of course we will hate in ourselves anything that displeases the Lord. The natural response to such recognition is repentance. In one sense, if I as a believer sin against God, it is true to say that he has already forgiven me – before I ask, before I have even done the wicked deed. But if I say "I won't bother to ask forgiveness because I am already forgiven," I am expressing a wrong attitude toward sin. That kind of thinking does not recognise the ugliness of sin in God's sight, its seriousness, etc. When we sin, we should hate it, not dismiss it with an easy theological shrug.

4. And of course, even after God forgives our sins against him, we continue to need forgiveness for our sins against our fellow human beings. Jesus teaches us in Matt 5 and 18 that we should be quick to seek reconciliation. It would be wrong, when I sin against another person, to say, "well, God has forgiven me, so I don't care about reconciling with you." P

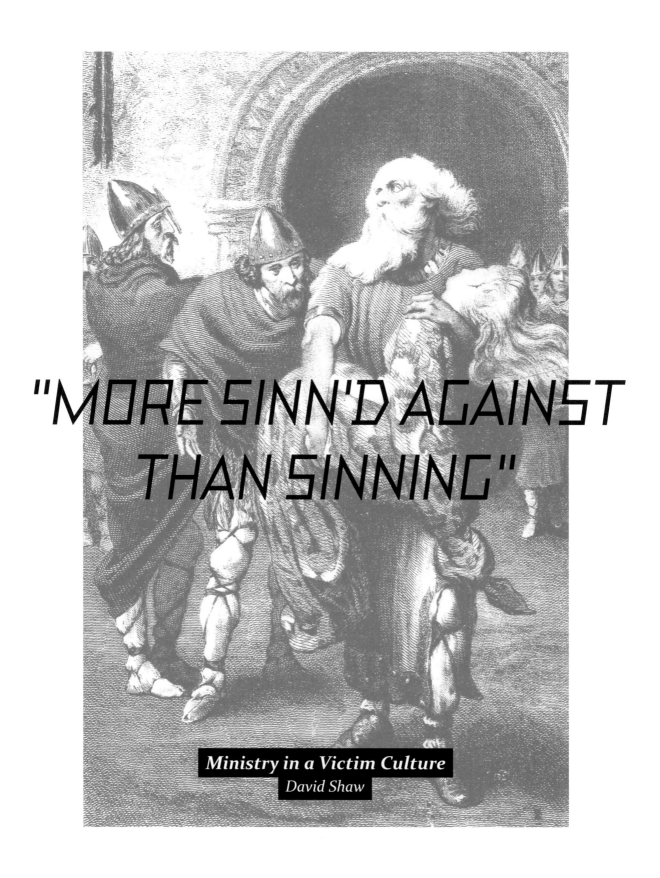

"MORE SINN'D AGAINST THAN SINNING"

Ministry in a Victim Culture
David Shaw

I want to begin with Jeremy Clarkson and King Lear. An odd couple I admit, but bear with me.

In Act 3 scene 2 King Lear is on a downward spiral – he has treated his three daughters rather badly and has been treated worse by two of them in return – and now in the midst of a wild storm he declares himself to be *"a man more sinn'd against than sinning."*

Looking back on his own recent stormy past, Jeremy Clarkson has made a similar declaration. Below a Telegraph headline – *Jeremy Clarkson lays bare his tempestuous relationship with senior BBC executives* – we read that "the former Top Gear host accuses senior managers investigating allegations of racism at a time when he was emotionally vulnerable." The article ends in a similar vein: "Asked to describe the year, Clarkson added: 'In one year I lost my mother, my house, my job. How do you think I felt?'" The question hangs but the implication is clear. Jeremy is a man *more sinn'd against than sinning*. Indeed in the whole article there is no acknowledgment that he did anything wrong at all. He is the unfortunate victim of unfeeling managers.

telegraph.co.uk/news/bbc/12198568/ Jeremy-Clarkson-lays-bare-his- tempestuous-relationship-with- senior-BBC-executives.html

It's a bold manoeuvre, for someone who has gleefully offended so many people and who was fired for physically attacking a colleague, but in truth it's one that we are all tempted to make. To look back on the past and to rewrite the story as if we were the ones sinned against, and others were to blame.

This scramble to be seen as a victim is an increasingly prevalent way of dealing with conflict or guilt. Indeed, the Clarkson story is just one snapshot of what is often referred to as an emerging 'victim culture.' Sometimes the victim is a role we'll just adopt in extreme situations, but often it can be a more settled view of the world and what's wrong with it.

Alan Mann describes the basic outlook:

> *As the victim we are helpless, the casualty of social structures, institutions and corporate bodies. It is with them that responsibility lies, not with the innocent victim of their distorted practices.*

Alan Mann, *Atonement for a "Sinless" Society: Engaging with an Emerging Culture* (Milton Keynes: Authentic Media, 2005), 25.

Does that sound familiar? All we need to do is supply the "them." Senior Management, Bankers, Tories, Socialists, the Establishment, Etonian toffs, the EU, the Police, Social Services, the Media. The well never runs dry.

As people have observed these trends, they have raised a number of concerns that start to help us reflect on the impact of victim culture.

See e.g. The Moral Maze on "Victim Culture" (BBC Radio 4, 17th June 2015); Arthur C. Brooks, "The Real Victims of Victimhood," *The New York Times*, December 26, 2015; Conor Friedersdorf, "The Rise of Victimhood Culture," *The Atlantic*, September 11, 2015. Neil Davenport, "Why Victim Culture Is Running Riot," *Spiked*, July 10, 2012, www.spiked-online.com/newsite/article/riot_church/12618

THE IMPACT OF A VICTIM CULTURE

First, this mindset is incredibly *divisive*, as Arthur Brooks observes it in the political sphere:

Brooks, "The Real Victims of Victimhood."

Victimhood makes it more and more difficult for us to resolve political and social conflicts. The culture feeds a mentality that crowds out a necessary give and take – the very concept of good-faith disagreement – turning every policy difference into a pitched battle between good (us) and evil (them).

It is also *paralysing*, as John Humphrys observes:

John Humphrys, *Devil's Advocate* (London: Arrow, 2000), 18, from the opening chapter "The Victim Culture."

One of the things about being a victim is that even if you can't blame someone for the condition you're in, you can hold them responsible for getting you out of it.

All too often, if we start seeing ourselves as victims we take on a passive role: helpless in the situation because of the actions of others, and helpless afterwards until someone else comes along to fix the situation. Tragically this paralysis can often deepen the divisiveness as well – we can blame other people for our mess *and* complain about them bitterly until the problem gets fixed.

Third, some research has found that a victim mentality is also *corrupting*. An intriguing experiment in the Psychology Department of Stanford University in the US asked half of the students participating to remember a time when they were bored and the other half to remember a time when they felt something unfair had happened to them. They were then asked how willing they would be to help in future experiments and how strongly they agreed with statements like "I deserve more things in my life," "things

Emily M. Zitek et al., "Victim Entitlement to Behave Selfishly," *Journal of Personality and Social Psychology 98*, no. 2 (2010), 245-55.

should go my way," and "I am entitled not to suffer too much." The results showed that the students who had recalled an unfair experience were "significantly less likely" to help in the future and rated their entitlement to happiness higher.

In a subsequent experiment the researchers designed a game in which some people lost fairly, simply because the game was hard, and others lost unfairly because the computer crashed. They were then asked how future prize money should be allocated, and those who'd experienced the "unfair" situation proved far more likely to award themselves a larger share of future winnings. In one very striking aside, the authors of the study noted that students who'd remembered or experienced something unfair were more likely even to leave rubbish on the desks and steal the experimenters' pens. In the words of the scientists' summary, "Our research has shown that people who have just been wronged or reminded of a time when they were wronged feel entitled to positive outcomes, leading them to behave selfishly. They no longer feel obligated to suffer for others and therefore pass up opportunities to be helpful."

ibid., 253.

In various ways then our society is observing and lamenting this shift towards a culture of victimhood and entitlement. And for obvious reasons, the way that this mindset allows people to shift responsibility onto others matters for us as Christians. The gospel message requires that people admit their own guilt in order to receive forgiveness and new life in Christ. More widely, this mindset is infecting the society in which we live and easily penetrates the life of the church as well. For those reasons we will spend a bit of time digging deeper into this victim mentality. We begin with the help of an essay by Mike Ovey called *'Victim chic? The rhetoric of victimhood.'*

Michael J. Ovey, "Victim Chic? The Rhetoric of Victimhood," *Cambridge Papers* (2006), www.jubilee-centre.org/victim-chic-the-rhetoric-of-victimhood-by-michael-ovey/

The first thing to be said, of course, is that there are genuine victims and genuine persecutors. We will focus on the ways in which we *claim* a victim status but as Mike reminds us, some people genuinely are the "undeserved target of another's action" (victims). Others target individuals or groups without warrant to do them harm (persecutors). This is a tragic and all too common experience in a fallen world. Furthermore, as we will go on to say, most situations are far more complicated than a simple allocation of victim/persecutor roles will allow. For now, though, the point is that we very often deny these complex realities, oversimplifying things in self-serving ways.

THE DYNAMICS OF A VICTIM CULTURE

The original study is Stephen Karpman, 'Fairy Tales and Script Drama Analysis,' *Transactional Analysis Bulletin 7*, 1968: 39-43.

Depending on the version you read she's either in the cupboard or the wolf's stomach by the time Little Red Riding Hood knocks on her door.

For an analytical tool, Mike draws on a study of fairy tale narratives which describes a 'victim triangle' arranged around three roles: Victim, Persecutor, Rescuer. Take, for example, *Little Red Riding Hood* and, leaving aside poor Grandma for a moment, we can map out the end of the story like this:

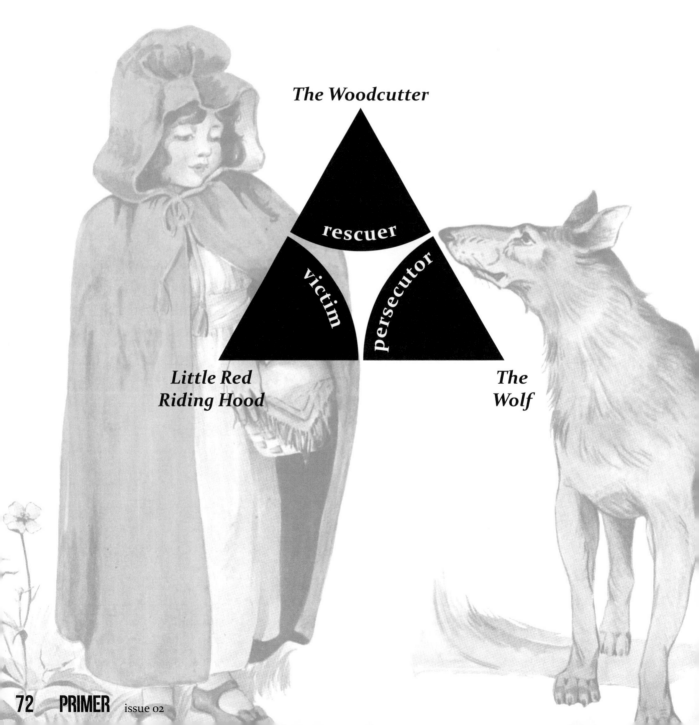

The Woodcutter

rescuer

victim

persecutor

Little Red Riding Hood

The Wolf

In the context of the story, that assignment of roles reflects the truth of the matter. But the point is that we can take all three roles and creatively reassign them to suit ourselves.

So for example, in any given conflict, there might genuinely be fault on both sides but we cast ourselves as the victim and attribute *all* guilt to the person we've cast as our persecutor.

Or we can respond to someone else's feelings of victimisation by appointing ourselves their champions and rescuers. That makes us feel good, and it can suit the 'victim' to have someone reinforce their identification as such.

We can also exploit someone's genuine victimhood and appoint ourselves as their rescuer in ways that serve our own egos and agendas.

Taking that point further, we can encourage someone to feel victimised in order to cast someone we are hostile towards as persecutor and so legitimise attacking them. That is, we can be a persecutor masquerading as a rescuer. If we can spin the situation that way the advantages are obvious: both 'victim' and 'rescuer' are free from any real accountability because within that narrative their cause is righteous and the 'persecutor' is just getting what they deserve. No-one feels sorry for the wolf.

How do you see this being worked out in your context? In the wider culture? What examples can you think of?

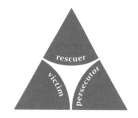

How can this affect relationships in church life? Ministry? Marriage?

ENGAGING A VICTIM CULTURE
WITH SCRIPTURE

How then does the Bible's teaching about sin connect with a victim culture? From one perspective the culture presents an obvious challenge – how do we communicate the reality of sin to a world so skilled in passing the buck? On the other hand, this victim culture actually offers two insights on the nature of sin.

1. More briefly, victim culture illustrates how all sin is a failure to love God and love our neighbour. In relation to our neighbours, we have already seen how we can leverage past or present sufferings to justify acting selfishly towards others. Furthermore, the act of casting others as our persecutors means that we treat them as categorically different to us. They are evil, we are just. That means, to state the obvious, that we won't love them as our neighbour. Instead we demonise them.

   Victim culture is also, crucially, a failure to love God, for the act of identifying myself as victim is an attempt to usurp God's authority as judge. As Mike Ovey notes, "conferring self-righteousness on myself is a sovereign judicial act. I define myself and who and what I am. This readily looks like establishing my own identity and nature independently of God." Furthermore, by acting as the casting director and assigning roles to other people we encroach even further on God's authority: he alone is the judge of other people's actions and motives.

   Ovey, "Victim Chic?"

2. In doing this I am also constructing an alternative reality. This is the second major lesson to learn about sin from our victim culture. The stories we tell about ourselves as victims show us how delusional and deceptive sin can be. Sin is not just a matter doing wrong things, rather it corrupts our knowledge of God and ourselves. It means we live in a kind of unreality.

   This is borne out in several scenes of temptation and sin in the Bible. Just think for a moment about the temptation scene in Genesis 3. What are the true roles in Genesis 3? Well, as the serpent brings the temptation he is the persecutor, Adam is the victim and God, ideally, is the rescuer Adam would turn to in the midst of temptation. But which roles do Adam and Eve assign to God and the serpent? They buy into the serpent's alternative reality. They start to see God as their persecutor – he is the one who is not telling the truth ("You will not certainly die" Gen 3:4) and the one who is keeping good things from them ("For God knows that when you eat from it your eyes will be opened, and you will be like God, knowing good and evil." Gen 3:5). And so they treat the serpent as a rescuer – the one who is on their side. After the fall Adam persists in that unreality, playing the innocent victim and continuing to treat God as the persecutor, laying the blame at God's door: "The woman *you* put here with me – she gave me some fruit from the tree, and I ate it."

Or take a look at Numbers 14:1-9. Here is Israel grumbling in the wilderness. God has brought them out of Egypt. He has rescued them from the hands of their persecutor Pharoah. He is leading them to the promised land and the spies have testified to the goodness of what's in store. And yet notice the alternative reality Israel starts to create. God is their persecutor: "Why is the Lord bringing us to this land only to let us fall by the sword? Our wives and children will be taken as plunder" (14:3). And where do they turn for rescue? "Wouldn't it be better for us to go back to Egypt?" And they said to each other, "We should choose a leader and go back to Egypt" (14:3-4).

In both temptation scenes Adam and Israel sin in their unbelief and rejection of God. Instead of continuing to trust God's word and his promises, they give in to temptation. For our purposes what is so striking is the story they tell: God is against us, we are innocent, someone else is our rescuer. This is not just an alternative reality, it is an anti-reality, an utter denial of the truth about God that lies at the heart of every sin. Adam and Eve protest their innocence even after they have sinned and they continue in sin and unbelief by persisting with the lie that God is at fault and they are innocent. Likewise the Israelites were showing themselves to have hearts "hardened by sin's deceitfulness" when they recast God as their persecutor in the wilderness (Heb 3:13). So when we sin we show that we don't truly love God or our neighbour, but it's also true that when we sin we show we don't truly know God or ourselves. Sin is delusional.

Victim culture is nothing new then. It's a constant feature of humanity's response to God. See e.g. Psalm 2 where the rulers of the earth cast God as the one who enslaves and enchains them:

The kings of the earth rise up
  and the rulers band together
  against the LORD and against his anointed, saying,
*"Let us break their chains
  and throw off their shackles."*

"IN TODAY'S THERAPEUTIC AGE, THE CULTURAL SCRIPT IS... AN UNAPPEALING MIX OF GROSS EMOTIONAL INCONTINENCE AND AGGRESSIVE ASSERTIONS OF VICTIMISATION. EVEN WITHOUT OCEANS OF BOOZE INSIDE THEM, I'VE SEEN YOUNG PEOPLE KICK OFF IN PUBLIC – TO BUS INSPECTORS CHECKING TICKETS OR SHOPKEEPERS, FOR EXAMPLE – USING THE THERAPEUTIC LANGUAGE OF ASSERTIVE VICTIMHOOD."

Neil Davenport, "Why Victim Culture Is Running Riot," Spiked, July 10, 2012,

IMPLICATIONS FOR THE CHURCH

1. We need to beware of casting ourselves or the church as victims of society

Of course this is complicated by the fact that there is genuine persecution of Christians, to some extent in the UK and certainly across much of the world. In those situations of course the Bible holds out great hope for victims of persecution. As we participate in the sufferings of Jesus (1 Pet 4:13), we can sing the psalms with him and commit ourselves to the Father as he did, knowing that he upholds his children and will repay their enemies (Rom 12:19-20).

On the other hand, we do need to beware of the mindset of a victim culture.

- ➡ It is founded on the premise that we are entitled not to suffer and that every hardship ought to be resolved. This is simply not the experience of God's people in this life.

- If we embrace a victim mentality we can be tempted to forget who our true rescuer is and appeal, as so many groups do, to the State for its protection. Again this is complicated because the State does have a God-given role to uphold justice and the cause of the oppressed. And yet politicians very often set themselves up as saviours/rescuers in ways we must resist. So we need to remember who our true rescuer is or else our hopes will be severely misplaced and frequently dashed. "Do not put your trust in princes, in human beings, who cannot save" (Psalm 146:3).

- The other danger is that we can set up an 'us and them' mentality with the world which jeopardises our love for the lost. As we've seen, the 'victim triangle' relies on demonising those who persecute you, rather than praying for them (Matt 5:44) or blessing them (Rom 12:14).

2. We need to beware of allowing a victim culture in church

This is true both for how we relate to God and to one another. As Hebrews 3-4 makes clear, there is a very real danger that we repeat Israel's mistake when we are faced with hardship and suffering by grumbling against God. We need to recognise the deceitfulness of sin that encourages us to re-narrate our circumstances and to harbour bitterness against God for them. We need to recognise that God uses hardship as a means to refine and bless us and to teach us to depend on him (2 Cor 1:9).

Proactively, that means we need to teach about and model a faithful response to temptation, disappointment and suffering.

We have also seen that central to those temptation scenes is the willingness to recast God as the one who is against us. Therefore, we will serve people well by helping them see the beauty and goodness of God's ways. We need to help people entrust themselves to their Father's care the way the Son does faced with his temptation (Luke 4:1-13).

As for our inter-personal relationships, pastoral wisdom by the bucketload is crucial. In most conflict situations the reality is that people have sinned *and* have been sinned against. But we will meet some people who have been terribly victimised and will be carrying a burden of guilt when they bear no responsibility for what has happened to them. On the other hand, we will meet people who are projecting all responsibility onto others and casting themselves as victims. In relation to that latter group we must not collude with them. It can be tempting to do so and adopt the role of rescuer at that point. If we do, joining with them in saying how terribly they've been treated, they will embrace us, but we need to bring reality to bear. All too often that means we find ourselves quickly moved from the 'rescuer' to 'persecutor' category in their minds, but so be it.

"THE RESULT OF THIS RELIGION OF RIGHTS IS THAT PEOPLE FEEL UNENDINGLY HARD DONE BY. EVERY DISAPPOINTMENT IS MET WITH A LAWSUIT, IN THE HOPE OF TURNING MATERIAL LOSS TO MATERIAL GAIN. AND WHATEVER HAPPENS TO US, WE OURSELVES ARE NEVER AT FAULT."

Roger Scruton, *Gentle Regrets: Thoughts from a Life* (London: Bloomsbury, 2006), 236.

IMPLICATIONS FOR EVANGELISM

1. We need to help people see that there are false rescuers out there and point them to Jesus

As we noted above, some individuals or organisations encourage people to see themselves as victims in order to set themselves up as rescuers, and yet they are very often preying on those they claim to champion. They are idols in search of worshippers but they cannot save.

2. We need to help people see they are not innocent victims and point them to Jesus

It is not simply a matter of helping people to realise that they have sought rescue in the wrong place and pointing them to Jesus. We need to help people to see that we are all guilty of rejecting God and spurning his goodness. We need to help people feel the offence of casting God as the one who seeks to deprive us of good things when he is the one who has generously lavished good gifts on us. We also need to help people take responsibility for many of the problems in their lives that they project onto others and for the ways in which they victimise others.

As we do so it's important that we don't deny the reality of the external factors that people will be tempted to blame for everything. Indeed, one of the virtues of the Bible's account of sin is that it knows exactly how complicated life is. The human predicament does involve enemies without and enemies within, but crucially these do not absolve us of responsibility. Ephesians 2:1-4 is adamant about that – we were objects of wrath and disobedient, even while we were influenced by the course of the world and were acted upon by the ruler of the kingdom of the air. Indeed sin can be described as a power that enslaves us (see John 8, Romans 6) and yet we cannot claim to have been innocent victims. As Richard Hays writes:

Richard B. Hays, *The Moral Vision of the New Testament: Community, Cross, New Creation, A Contemporary Introduction to New Testament Ethics* (Edinburgh: T&T Clark, 1996), 390.

The Bible's sober anthropology rejects the apparently commonsense assumption that only freely chosen acts are morally culpable. Quite the reverse: the very nature of sin is that it is not freely chosen. That is what it means to live "in the flesh" in a fallen creation. We are in bondage to sin but still accountable to God's righteous judgment of our actions.

How then do we try to bring this complex reality to bear on people's lives? With prayer, certainly. No gospel explores the delusional aspect of sin better than John's Gospel, as Jesus engages with unbelievers who are incapable of seeing Jesus for who he is or themselves for who they are. In that context, Jesus' promise that the Holy Spirit will bring conviction to the world about sin, righteousness and judgment is a wonderful encouragement to dependence on him in our evangelism. Through Jesus' power people are transformed and the delusion of sin is ended. We can love God and our neighbour, we can know God and ourselves.

Beyond that, three final thoughts to help persuade people:

We can show people how the Christian worldview both challenges and affirms the assumptions behind a victim mindset.

I'm grateful to Stephen Lloyd for highlighting this argument.

Several times we've connected victim culture with the thought that 'I am entitled not to suffer.' It can be helpful to examine that assumption. On the one hand we can press people to justify it – how can a naturalistic worldview support such a claim? Doesn't Darwinianism depend on victims and don't we have to simply accept our place in the mechanisms of evolution? On the other hand, the Bible affirms the wrongness of suffering. It gives an account for why suffering is present in the world but it also holds out the promise of a new creation without suffering. One day the wolf will lie down with the lamb. And the Grandma.

We can help people feel the dignity of taking responsibility for their actions.

There is something profoundly paralysing and dehumanising about the victim culture. For all that people will think they are well-served by casting blame onto others and pretending they are simply the casualties of others' actions, there is a dignity in seeing our own actions as morally significant and taking responsibility for them.

We can show them the gospel holds out far more hope than a victim culture.

If people do start to take responsibility for their actions they will have to acknowledge that their moral story is one in which they are victimiser as well as victim. At this point they will need a better salvation than the one victim culture offers, for in a victim culture there is only redemption for those who can successfully claim the role of victim. Victimisers, on the other hand, are shut out, excluded, condemned. And yet the beauty of the gospel is that its salvation extends to victimisers like us. That's one angle by which we can preach the gospels and Acts as very countercultural and hope-filled stories: Jesus invites himself to dine with tax collectors – those oppressors of the people; he promises to bring thieves on crosses into his kingdom; He even seeks out his persecutor Saul (Acts 9:4) in order to be his rescuer. P